A Smattering Of Ignorance

OSCAR LEVANT

A Smattering
Of Ignorance

1940

DOUBLEDAY, DORAN & CO., INC., NEW YORK

PRINTED AT THE *Country Life Press*, GARDEN CITY, N. Y., U. S. A.

To
IRVING KOLODIN
With whose considerable aid
I have augmented my influence
and
diminished the circle of
my acquaintances

Contents

[vii]

CONTENTS

Introduction

MAY I ADD ONE ANECDOTE TO THE WON-
derful ones with which Oscar's book is crammed? We
met for dinner one night and I led him on—somewhat
as the sightseer leads on Niagara—to tell me his day. He
had run into a mutual acquaintance and had walked
along with him, he said, in pleasant converse. "I found
him agreeable and intelligent," said Oscar. I was
amazed. Was not that fellow Oscar's special antipathy?
Had he not only the other day covered him in con-
tumely? "I thought you hated him," I summarized.
Oscar made a quick, shamed-faced defence: "Well,
you know I hate 'em till they say hello to me." Some
people might find it less simple than that to undermine
Oscar's truculence but the anecdote is revealing.

I must tell another. One night Oscar called me to tell me that he had been fired from a radio job and was blue. I met him and we walked up Broadway. It was middle of winter, Oscar hatless and coatless, a shambling Mercutio, regarding with a dejected inner eye his multi-lit world. A young man stopped him with an effusive greeting. Oscar was not cordial. The young man, a lyric writer, did his best to pump up enthusiasm for some project on which he and Oscar had been engaged. There was no answering enthusiasm. Oscar left him abruptly. We walked away. I asked Oscar who the fellow was. "That's my protégé," said Oscar. "You did not wrap him in affection," I pointed out. "When I've just been fired," said Oscar, "I don't feel like being a patron!"

I don't know why I tell these two particular anecdotes. One, I suppose, because it reveals a substratum in Oscar's nature which arouses the maternal impulse in his men friends, whatever it may arouse in his lady ones; the other, I suppose, because it conveys somehow a hard-bitten integrity in Oscar which if it does not spare his friends, does not spare himself either. In any case, there is about Oscar a fabulous quality which makes it possible, in fact inevitable, once his name is mentioned, to discuss him for hours when he is not present. To say that Oscar is provocative would be putting it too mildly; he is practically a compulsion! As you can't always take him and you can never leave him, many of his friends find themselves for a long period in a state of uncomfortable abeyance like Dante's Limbo, until they finally decide that the tranquillity of an Oscarless life has only a negative compensation. All Oscar has to do in turn is to say hello to *them* and they melt, forget and forgive and return blissfully to the spiked embrace of his friendship. Whatever irritations they may have felt, they know they are happy to be back and are grateful because life is vivid and exciting and full of entertainment once more.

I must confess to a certain sadness on reading this book. It is not only that the most gifted of the band is gone—the piece on Gershwin, by the way, seems to me a unique and wonderful elegiac exercise—but because the middle-aged reader and occasional participant must realize that these pages are in a sense an In Memoriam to the part of his life that had in it the most unadulterated fun. Many, I am sure, who read this book will feel that it is also a record of their last fling at youth. With Oscar they forgot they were not as young as he is and would not be as young so long, but there must be a great many people who don't know Oscar (though that is hard to believe when you take a walk with him in almost any city) and for them this should be a happy introduction to a character who, if he did not exist, could not be imaged. That effort they will be spared for this book does reveal Oscar, a something new and completely "underivative" in his humor and point of view, in his integrity also. It is in the light of this penumbra-less integrity that Oscar sees himself as well as his friends and it is this visibility which makes his own stories about himself so awfully funny. For instance, when he was arranging his forthcoming concert appearances in Pittsburgh—— But I mustn't tell any more stories about Oscar. They must wait for the sequel to this book.

S. N. BEHRMAN

[xi]

Music In Aspic

Music In Aspic

IT HAS BEEN FREQUENTLY REMARKED, and with truth, that a conductor embarking on a debut in New York is confronted with the most critical audience in the world; save that this should be amended to read—at his first rehearsal. Long before a symphonic conductor appears before an audience to impress his qualities on the listeners, critical and otherwise, he has already made the impression that eventually determines the extent of his success or failure—on the members of the orchestra, whose atti-

[3]

control of an orchestra is most frequently founded on the less gaudy basis of economics. When an orchestra is aware that the conductor has in his inside pocket a contract for next season and the one after that, carrying with it the power to rearrange the personnel "for the best interests of the orchestra"— in other words, to hire and to fire—its attitude is apt to be somewhat more respectful than if he is merely an interloper to be tolerated for a brief guest engagement.

When Stokowski spent his memorable and brief guest engagement with the Philharmonic some years ago (as part of the famous exchange in which Toscanini conducted the Philadelphia Orchestra) he certainly did not leave his "authority," "beat" and "knowledge of scores" in the green room with his topcoat. But no one who recalls the occurrence will forget the playing of the Philharmonic which led Stokowski to describe the two weeks as one of the unhappiest experiences of his life.

To be sure, he made the initial mistake of asking the orchestra to learn, for the first time in its history, Stravinsky's "Sacre du Printemps," a work not previously in its repertory. This exertion, coupled with the orchestra's desire—at that time—to have Toscanini emerge as victor in the competition, induced a state of extreme resentment and internal opposition. This attitude was encouraged to no small extent by Stokowski's request, on beginning the rehearsal, for "one-hundred-per-cent co-operation." As one member of the orchestra says, "Well, you know, after all— a hundred-per-cent co-operation . . ." as though to say, "Who does he think he is, anyway?"

He also indicated his preference for absolute silence from the men when he was giving instructions to a particular choir or soloist. This was in effect an open invitation for whispers and privately exchanged jokes. When one of the bass players had the effontery to smile during a Stokowskian monologue he was summarily banished from the rehearsal. Expecting contriteness, Stokowski was astounded to hear him say, "Thank you—I haven't had a Thursday evening off all winter." This witticism evoked a giggle from a rear desk cellist, who was promptly directed to join his colleague in exile.

Plainly, neither of these occurrences would have happened in Philadelphia, where Stokowski exacts his "one hundred per cent co-operation" not merely by will power, his beautiful hands and exquisite gestures, but, more pertinently, through the players' knowledge

[7]

that dismissal from a rehearsal is not for a day or a week, but for all time.

It is hardly surprising, therefore, that present-day orchestral players in the more prominent ensembles have become almost as great prima donnas as the "glamour boys" of music whom they derisively decorate with that epithet. There is the charming and somewhat pathos-tinged experience of Bruno Walter's during one of his first guest appearances with the Philharmonic. Innocent and unwarned, he had endured for several rehearsals and the first pair of concerts the mannerisms of Alfred Wallenstein, the orchestra's brilliant first cellist, whose gaze was everywhere—on the music, in the hall, up at the ceiling—but not on Walter. Since the first cellist sits almost within baton's length of the conductor, his idiosyncrasy could hardly be overlooked.

At last, Walter invited him to a conference and said, "Tell me, Mr Wallenstein, what is your ambition?"

The cellist replied that he someday hoped to be a conductor.

"Well," said the conductor, with his sweet and patient smile, "I only hope you don't have Wallenstein in front of you."

In the relationship of conductor and orchestra much

depends of course on the first meeting. As a human equation, it has much the same atmosphere as the meeting of the principals in a prearranged Hungarian wedding, with the bride and groom thoroughly aware that they are fated to make common cause whether they are enamored of each other or not. These are not marriages made in heaven; they are made mostly in the office of Mr Arthur Judson.

The methods of approach by the conductor vary as widely as the literary tempers of Dale Carnegie's *How to Win Friends and Influence People* and Adolf Hitler's *Mein Kampf*. To this mating the orchestra brings suspicion, skepticism and mistrust in equal proportions. Unconsciously every conductor feels this and has developed a personal technique for breasting this psychological Maginot Line. With the less secure, the approach is invariably based on talk—a tribute to the magnificent musicianship of the band, a small disquisition on its splendid traditions (in whose future the conductor implies he hopes to play a part) and a sigh of anticipation for the pleasure the conductor expects to derive from playing on "this superb instrument." An appeal is made to the co-operative spirit of the men, together with an apostrophe to "what beautiful music we can make together." This is further known as the Clifford Odets or Gary Cooper-Madeleine Carroll approach, with the orchestra inclined to regard the conductor's part in the making of the beautiful music as perhaps an act of supererogation.

Violently opposed to this is approach II, the martinet or "knock-this-off-if-you-dare" type, in which the baton is, symbolically, a chip on the shoulder. Such a conductor invariably enters unexpectedly (thus immediately placing the orchestra at a disadvantage) clothed in a black half smock buttoned to the chin, providing a perfect stage setting for the indispensable Il Duce frown. No word of greeting is exchanged; a curt rap of the stick and a brisk command: "Beethoven." This the orchestra is expected to interpret to mean the symphony of the program. Further communication by word is withheld until the first mistake, no matter how slight. This provides the opportunity for which the conductor has been waiting to address a negative greeting to his co-workers, in which are mingled supercilious endearment and patronizing contempt.

Falling somewhere between these two is approach III—the good-fellow or Uriah Heep type. The conductor walks in calmly, clothed in a smile, shakes hands with the concertmaster, taps gently for attention and addresses the orchestra as "Gentlemen." A harmless, well-prepared joke follows, leading up to the suggestion that since they are going to be together for weeks and months it would be best to develop a "Just call me Al" entente cordial. Sometimes this flowers into a "mingling-with-the-help" manner: the conductor cultivates a program of socio-musical escapades with members of the orchestra, invites them to his home for chamber-music evenings and sponsors Christmas parties for the children of the musicians. His purpose is to efface the social (and monetary) disparities between conductor and players, to give them an illusion of fraternal equality, to cultivate the impression that he is "just one of the boys." This usually endures only for the first season, after which the chrysalis is discarded, and he emerges from the cocoon to try his wings as a martinet.

More to be pitied than censured is the nervous, irritable type, generally hired for only two weeks in the middle of the season and secretly convinced that the orchestra is out to get him. His problem is to conduct a *Blitzkrieg* against an audience for which the permanent conductor has just directed every sure-fire work in the standard repertory. He is much in the position of a batter who steps to the plate after the previous man has hit a home run with the bases full. Entering with hasty, energetic steps, he mounts the podium in a leap, snaps his fingers with brittle impatience and says, "Three measures before letter C." Before the musicians have a chance to open their scores or raise their instruments his right arm is describing arcs and angles. Naturally confusion ensues, and he is apt to smite his forehead in despair and expostulate, "I won't have it, I won't have it, I *won't* have it!"

In such circumstances the musicians are likely to reply, "Take your time, buddy."

A recent development in the post-Toscanini period is the fabulous-memory type. He is shrewd enough to realize that an orchestra is no longer impressed with a musician who uses a score for rehearsals and conducts only his concerts from memory, so he scorns the use of a score in his rehearsals also. He has memorized not only the notes and tempo indications, but also the numbers of the pages, the lettered subdivisions of the movements and even the accent marks in the bassoon part.

It is a part of orchestral folk legend that one such virtuoso, intent upon impressing the orchestra with his memory, planted several errors in obscure places. In the midst of a furious tutti he stopped the orchestra, singled out the third horn player and said, "Third horn, I heard you play a C. It should be a C-sharp."

The horn player responded with proper contempt, "Some jackass wrote in a C natural, but I know the piece backward, so I played it C-sharp as it should be."

Unquestionably the most pathetic of all conductorial types is the man who has risen from the ranks, who frequently combines in his indeterminate manner some elements of all these approaches. As a former member of the orchestra which he is now conducting, he is subconsciously aware that the musicians are only waiting for the end of the rehearsal to get off together and discuss his failings as he has discussed with them, innumerable times in the past, those of the conductors he has played under himself. His method of generating authority cannot adhere to any of the stereotyped categories, since his case is a special one in which he first has to convince himself of his authority before he can transmit it to the players. Another accessible pitfall is electicism, the risk of reproducing the effects or mannerisms of some distinguished predecessor, thereupon permitting the members of the orchestra to say that he got this bar from so-and-so, that bar from another so-and-so.

A conductor should reconcile himself to the realization that regardless of his approach or temperament the eventual result is the same—the orchestra will hate him. This is true—hold your breath—even of Toscanini.

When Willem Mengelberg first exercised his virile vocabulary and exciting personality on the men of the Philharmonic early in the 1920's their enthusiasm for the new conductor mounted quickly from eager acceptance to blind idolatry. Perhaps there was an influence in the fact that his predecessor had been Josef Stransky.

This devotion endured for several seasons until a dark cloud, in the form of Arturo Toscanini, appeared on the horizon. For some time the loyalty of the Mengelberg faction in the orchestra resisted the defection of the Toscanini cohorts, until it became apparent from the actions of the board and the public that the Mengelberg tenure was approaching its end. In the words of one of the players, "The boys knew there was a new boss coming in."—and Mengelberg was gleefully sabotaged. There was perhaps no organized plan, but, somehow, an orchestra which had played the first symphony of Beethoven times without number disagreed on the necessity for a repeat after the trio of the minuet. With the woodwinds espousing one opinion and the strings another, the helpless conductor found himself engulfed in dissonance.

In his turn, Toscanini passed through much the same cycle of endearment, questioning and resentment. There was rarely a cavil with his sincerity or extraordinary equipment, but his insistence on quality eventually won him the characterization which orchestral musicians apply to any intense and insatiable workman—"slave driver." This reached open rebellion during his last season, in the preparation of "Iberia" for an all-Debussy program at one of his final concerts. Contrary to the legend that Toscanini is unswervingly faithful to the smallest detail of a composer's conception, he felt that a horn passage in the coda required reinforcement by a trumpet and directed the incomparable Harry Glantz, first-chair man of that section, to play with the horns. Moreover, he specified that the addition be played forte. (Subsequently Glantz has given me many versions, one of which was that Reiner had introduced these changes in the parts previously.)

There was an unconscious reluctance on the musician's part, since he was accustomed to the sound of the original scoring, to play the note aggressively, and his forte was hardly more than a mezzo piano.

Toscanini interrupted the rehearsal and launched into a diatribe against Glantz, whose playing he had on many occasions praised. Angrily Glantz replied, "The trouble with you is you don't know how to handle men."

Such forthright opposition was unknown to Toscanini, and he stormily demanded an apology, whereupon Glantz walked out.

Unpredictably, the reaction in the orchestra was not sympathetic to Glantz. There was no feeling that he had been unjustified in his action, but they condemned the action on the eve of Toscanini's farewell from the orchestra. Shortly before, in the preparation of an all-Wagner program, the strings had resented Toscanini's demands for individual playing of a complex passage, impossible to play accurately, man by man, at any time, and sheer absurdity in their season-end state of nervous fatigue. They had discussed the possibilities of a strike, but agreed, as in the case of Glantz, that the time to take action was the year before—when Toscanini still had a power of dismissal over his men.

The difficulty between the two men was resolved by their mutual admiration—the fine musician for the peerless conductor, the demanding conductor for the irreplaceable musician. Through the mediation of Van Praag, manager of the orchestra personnel, an armistice was effected—without apology—for the duration of the concert. At its conclusion Glantz's magnificent performance won him a forgiving kiss on the cheek from the maestro.

Though it is commonly believed that a Toscanini performance is the highest reward a composer may expect for creating a work, it is an experience that sometimes has its embarrassing consequences. There was the time several years ago at a Philharmonic rehearsal when Ernest Schelling was present as soloist in the preparation of his "Impressions of an Artist's Life" for piano and orchestra. According to his custom, Toscanini was conducting without score while Schelling, the composer, had the music propped up on the rack before him.

The rehearsal progressed without incident for some minutes, then Toscanini, listening to Schelling expound a solo passage against a light orchestral background, suddenly rapped his stick imperiously on the stand beside him and called to Schelling, "What are you playing there?"

Schelling looked up in surprise and repeated the measures he had just played.

"No, no," said Toscanini. "Let me see the score."

He raised the score close to his eyes in the legendary way, peering intently at the page. Suddenly he looked up. "Just as I thought," he said. "You were playing wrong."

Schelling confirmed this astounding dictum by returning to the piano and playing a minutely different form of the passage he had just delivered. As he said afterward, he had always played it that way, never bothering to check it against the notes he had originally written.

Another example of Toscanini's remarkable musical faculties was the remark he made to Bernard Wagenaar, Dutch-American composer, after studying his first symphony for a performance of several years ago. Toscanini brought it back with him on a return trip from Europe, studying the score on the boat wholly by sight. When Wagenaar went to greet him at his hotel the day he arrived Toscanini congratulated him on the work but added, "There are several places which don't 'sound' "—a revelation that his memorization of the score included the ability to hear the actual *timbres* of the orchestra. The rehearsals revealed precisely the flaws in the texture of the scoring that he had predicted. This incident is in strong contrast to the opinion of others, who contend that only an actual playing will show the weaknesses of an orchestration. As a footnote to this it might be added that the dissonant conclusion of the first movement left Toscanini unsatisfied, and he insisted on adding a pure C-major chord to the composer's final page.

It is history, however, that one eminent contemporary felt otherwise than flattered by Toscanini's treatment of his music. This was the late Maurice Ravel, who was honored by a performance of his "Bolero" in Paris during the Philharmonic's European trip. It was an initial irritation for Ravel that no tickets had been sent to him, and he made his way into the crowded hall with great difficulty, to discover that Toscanini's tempo for "Bolero" was unforgivably fast. He added audible, unscored verbal comments from his box as the work progressed, in a mounting crescendo that paralleled the surge of the music. This monotone of invective brought a storm of shushing from the intent Parisians, to whom Ravel was not a world-famous composer but merely an ill-mannered listener.

The performance completed, Ravel descended angrily upon the green room to deliver his annoyance with the performance in person to the maestro. With voluble gestures and insistent pounding of his feet, he delineated the impossibility of dancing a "bolero," his or anyone else's, at such a pace. There was the charm of novelty in this experience for Toscanini, since only a composer of Ravel's stature could be thus indifferent to the maestro's reaction.

Despite this unprecedented experience Toscanini continued to conduct "Bolero," content, perhaps, to regard its unparalleled opportunity for orchestral virtuosity as compensation for the bad manners of the composer. After several brilliant performances with the Philharmonic, in which he had been delighted by the meticulous playing of the orchestra's percussion section, he summoned its members to his room and expressed his particular pleasure with the snare drummer, Schmehl, whose superb pianissimo and imperceptible crescendo excelled anything in his experience.

A large florid man with the muscularity of a heavyweight wrestler and a speech compounded equally of Brooklynese and Hemingway, Schmehl replied casually, "Tanks, boss—glad you feel that way about me."

The praise apparently aroused Schmehl to the difficulty of his task and a consciousness of how well he had accomplished it, for at the next repetition of "Bolero" he was swept by panic, beginning his opening solo at a rapidly increasing forte. A contortion of rage suffused Toscanini's face, and he muttered imprecations. Schmehl's partner sought to retrieve the sticks and play the solo himself, but the drummer was too nervous to understand the request. The fury of Toscanini with Schmehl transmitted itself to the rest of the orchestra, a trombone exploded a blast instead of a tone at the climax of his solo, and the performance moved swiftly into confusion.

When the final chord had been reached Toscanini stalked from the stage without a glance at the audience and rushed to his room, crying, "Where is Schmehl? I want Schmehl! *Send me Schmehl!*"

The culprit finally appeared, to be greeted by a torrent of "Stupido . . . Shame . . . You play no more for me!" All this to the man he had recently decorated with garlands of praise.

Truculently Schmehl accepted the abuse with the patience born of forty years' experience in orchestral playing and, waiting his opportunity, finally said, "You don't like my work? Get yourself another boy."

Nevertheless, it cost him his post in the orchestra for one misgauged pianissimo.

There might have been a similar outcome for another impasse at a Philharmonic rehearsal had not the player shrewdly adapted himself to one of Toscanini's few limitations. The problem arose in the rehearsing of Berlioz' "Queen Mab" scherzo (in the "Romeo and Juliet" music). This contains an effect scored for antique cymbals, the tiny equivalents of the familiar large cymbals. Toscanini demanded that the rapid tinkling of the instruments be mathematically precise and metronomically exact, the rhythm sharply articulated.

One after another the percussion players took their turns at attempting to meet Toscanini's requirements, only to find that the task of rustling the two tiny dials together at the proper speed and with the desired clarity defied any technique with which they were acquainted. They were all waved impatiently aside until Sam Borodkin, virtuoso of the gong, tam-tam, bass drum and glockenspiel, pushed his way to the stand and said he'd like to try.

The orchestra began, and Borodkin stood poised with the small cymbals (each no larger than a silver dollar) in his hands. When his entrance approached Borodkin bent over the stand in an attitude of extreme attentiveness, meanwhile substituting a metal triangle stick for the cymbal in his right hand. Then, with his hands barely visible over the top of the stand, he beat out the rhythm perfectly.

Toscanini dropped his baton and called out, "Bravo, Borodkin, bravo"—being unable to penetrate the deception with his weak vision. No doubt if he could have seen that far he would have found some reason to be displeased with the results.

It is such arbitrary and unpredictable attitudes that exhaust the patience of men who feel that their status, tried and approved, entitles them to better treatment. In this genre there is the classic experience of the violinist Mischel ("Mike") Gussikoff, who was engaged as concertmaster of the Philadelphia Orchestra after Stokowski personally scouted his playing of the solo violin part of Strauss's "Ein Heldenleben" with the St Louis Symphony. When the orchestra assembled to begin its season Gussikoff took his place at the first desk but noticed that Stokowski did not shake hands with him, greet him by name or even nod.

This situation endured not only for the first rehearsal, but through the week's concerts and for all of the next month. Eventually Gussikoff began to worry about this silent relationship with Stokowski and sought to identify it with possible flaws in his playing. He could not find any that justified such mute indictment, and in final desperation he sought out Stokowski during a train trip from a New York concert and said, "Please, Dr Stokowski, I have done something to displease you?"

"No," said the conductor.

"You don't like the way I play my solos?"

"I have no complaint," said Stokowski.

"Then why," questioned Gussikoff, "why don't you *say* something to me?"

"When I say something," answered Stokowski, "that will be the time to worry."

Baffled by this negative endorsement, Gussikoff withdrew and shortly afterwards found himself a position with another orchestra.

It is possible that Gussikoff reacted with particular sensitivity because he had been reared in the prewar Russian Symphony Orchestra, under the genial guidance of Modest Altschuler. This was the orchestra that was a veritable training school for concertmasters, producing, among others, Frederic Fradkin (of the Boston Symphony), Maxmilian Pilzer (of the Philharmonic), Ilya Skolnik (of the Detroit Symphony), Louis Edlin (of the National Orchestral Association), and the conductors Nikolai Sokoloff and Nat Finston (of the movies). It was this orchestra that introduced many of the finest scores by Scriabin, Rachmaninoff and Stravinsky (his first symphony and "L'Oiseau de

Feu" particularly outraging the Krehbiels and Fincks)
to New York long before the established orchestras
were aware of their existence.

An ardent propagandist for such works, Altschuler
also delighted in expounding his conceptions of the
scores with illustrated lectures. Attempting to elicit a
more soulful solo from his oboist in a rehearsal of
"Scheherazade," he stopped and said, "Here is the
princess (pointing to the concertmaster, who plays
the overfamous violin cadenza) and you are making
love to her." Then, studying the pimpled complexion
of the violinist, he added, "I'm sorry I can't do better."

Life in this orchestra was much like attendance at
a private university. Such men as Harry Glantz, the
admired first trumpet of the Philharmonic, had their
early training in the German school of playing almost
wholly revised under Altschuler's guidance. When
the orchestra toured—as it frequently did—the travels
resembled a mass picnic, with baskets of native deli-
cacies ranging from salamis to cheeses carted along as
sustenance against the barbaric foods to be found
inland.

Such an organization could not fail to produce its
quota of legend, of which several stories concerned a
typical tour during which two Russian violinists,

desk mates in the orchestra, who also traveled together, and shared a hotel room wherever the orchestra played, were met with the query by the clerk:

"Do you want a room with bath?"

They looked at each other blankly until one could finally find the words to say,

"Who wants a bath? We're only going to be here a week."

When they had disposed of their belongings and come down to the hotel dining room most of their colleagues had already eaten. Seeing one still left in the room, they sauntered over and inquired, "What's good? What did you have to eat?"

The friend replied, "I had the chicken potpie. Very tasty."

When the waiter appeared they both placed orders for the chicken pie.

"I'm sorry," he replied. "We're all out of it."

The articulate one studied the menu for a moment and then said, "All right, then bring me the deep-dish apple pie."

It was in this orchestra, its scattered survivors of today claim, that there originated the fable that has since been attributed to every musical organization that gives outdoor concerts, from the Philharmonic

Orchestra to the Goldman Band. They were playing the "Leonore No. 3" overture of Beethoven during a summer engagement, and the first trumpeter had stolen from his place to give the off-stage fanfare heralding the approach of the Minister of Justice.

Retreating an appropriate distance from the orchestra stand, he raised his instrument, waited for the cue and was just about to blow when a park policeman rushed up and bellowed, "You can't do that here! Don't you know there's a concert going on?"

Regardless of their respect for a conductor's musicianship or their admiration for his interpretative gifts, an orchestra is as frequently made uncomfortably aware of his feet of clay as they are of his head in the clouds. Several seasons ago, according to legend, the men of the Philadelphia Orchestra were baffled by Stokowski's desire to conduct, at one of his final rehearsals of the regular season, Strauss's "Blue Danube" waltz. It was not scheduled to be played at any remaining concert of the year, and the conductor's meticulous preparation of the score, his insistence on this effect and that phrasing, could only be interpreted as a whim.

The incident had passed from their minds by the time they reassembled to play their summer series of concerts at Robin Hood Dell, of which the first was conducted by a guest. Following the intermission the chairman appeared before the audience, thanked the listeners for their attendance and added, "Perhaps you have not noticed that we have among us tonight a distinguished guest—our beloved Dr Stokowski. I know you would be delighted to have him conduct something for us this evening."

Stokowski resisted the flattery with gestures of un-assuming modesty, listened to the applause and finally indicated that he was powerless to deny the audience its wish. He mounted the stage and suggested that the librarian distribute the parts of "The Blue Danube."

Occasionally, and at widely separated intervals, a musician will give forth an opinion based not only on his reaction to a given situation, but summing up in sparse phrases his reaction to a conductor's whole personality. When such an incident occurs it is pre-served not merely for its succinctness but also for its assertiveness, enduring as part of the folk legend of orchestral players.

A famous incident of that nature involved, by co-incidence, two musicians almost miraculously opposed in size, type and temperament—the six-foot-four Otto Klemperer, probably the tallest conductor extant, and the barely five-foot Bruno Labate, diminutive oboe virtuoso of the Philharmonic Symphony Orchestra. It is traditional that orchestral conductors follow one of two practices in their rehearsals of standard works. Generically, conductors of the German school will begin a work, say Beethoven's "Eroica," and play it methodically from beginning to end, indicating as they progress their preferences in dynamics, accents and phrasings. Others, particularly English and French conductors, in order to expedite rehearsals during a brief guest engagement, will assume that an experienced orchestra is competent to deal with the large aspects of such a work without measure-by-measure supervision and merely rehearse those sections in which their ideas are personal—perhaps in the development or at the beginning of the recapitulation.

It is a trait of the thoroughgoing Klemperer to espouse *both* methods, beginning with the scattered-intensive and progressing thereafter to the over-all-intensive. This treatment he frequently interrupts, in the preparation of a Beethoven work, with discourses, say, on the metronome of Beethoven's time and the state of the composer's relations with his nephew Karl when the work was written, with perhaps even a

[29]

monologue on the alterations of pitch in the hundred years since.

Having completed such a discourse on one occasion, he turned to Ravel's "Le Tombeau de Couperin" and proceeded to dissect it, page by page, with particular attention to a rather difficult oboe phrase. Four times, five times, he asked to hear it, and even at the sixth playing he was not satisfied. Disregarding the difficulty an oboist has in controlling his breath for long stretches and the inevitable tiring of the player's lips, he asked for it again, pausing for a brief footnote on Ravel's use of the oboe before he raised his baton.

Labate peered over his stand at the mountainous conductor and pronounced the undying words, "Mr Klemps', you talka too much."

There was, of course, the inevitable demand for an apology. The indispensable Van Praag was taxed to the utmost of his considerable ingenuity in dealing with such situations. Perhaps Labate's outspokenness was based on the realization that motivated him when a co-worker, aghast at his ability to play perfectly any solo, no matter how complicated or unfamiliar, under the tension of concert conditions, asked him,

"Don't you *ever* get nervous?"

To which Labate answered with the assertion,

"Wit' sevent-five tousanda dollar in the bank, I no get nervous."

Such conflicts of personality are not limited to the common relationship of conductors and the men they conduct. When a soloist of individual temperament is preparing a concerto for performance, the conflict of personality is not limited to the conductor and the members of the orchestra, but sometimes becomes three sided.

When Toscanini was engaged in his Brahms cycle with the Philharmonic several seasons ago the soloist for the B-flat concerto was the late Ossip Gabrilowitsch. They came to the rehearsal with a remarkable disparity of experiences in relation to the work: Gabrilowitsch having played it with glory in every important musical center of the world and attained a highly personal and intimate understanding of its contents, Toscanini having never had the necessity to conduct it in public even once before. Nevertheless, Toscanini confronted the orchestra and the soloist with a firm, characteristically inflexible conception of its tempo, its nuances, its phrasing, in which Gabrilowitsch's preferences were hardly considered and of course not respected. When the bewildered soloist found himself approaching the work anew, almost recasting his whole conception, he sought to reason Toscanini to an understanding of his viewpoint. In this he was thoroughly unsuccessful. He gave up the crusade in despair, and the performance was canceled.

As recently as last winter the Philharmonic was party to another conflict of soloist and conductor when Artur Schnabel rehearsed the "Emperor" concerto of Beethoven with John Barbirolli. There was a substantial agreement between the two men on the main details of the performance, but as the rehearsals progressed it was apparent that the orchestra was being influenced by two conductors. Schnabel, as he played, not only nodded his approval of this orchestral soloist's phrasing of a certain passage or his admiration for the tone of another man, but he also extended a warning hand toward the orchestra when it produced more tone than he thought necessary and finally singled out the flutist John Amans for an admonishing,

"Too loud—too loud."

Barbirolli had no choice but to stop the orchestra and suggest to Schnabel that the soloist's desires should be expressed to him and not to the orchestra; that, after all, he was the conductor, and his authority was in jeopardy. Perhaps the conductor would have been more tolerant if his most celebrated excellence—his talent for directing accompaniments—was not, by implication, being questioned.

Musically, Schnabel's action was more appropriate to an operatic tenor than it was to the pianist widely admired as one of the most "scholarly" and musicianly interpreters of his specialty, Beethoven, now before the public. From the orchestra's standpoint Schnabel's behavior was wholly irrelevant and unethical and merely made them twice as eager to respect Barbirolli's wishes, if only as a condemnation of Schnabel's presumption.

As anyone who has had contact with orchestral players is aware, they are not occupationally allergic to authority save when it is misused. A professional, well-routined orchestra such as the Philharmonic or the Philadelphia can give a competent performance of a standard score regardless of who is directing it (as last summer's example of the Philharmonic under His Honor Fiorello H. LaGuardia testifies), but this is a procedure to be embraced only in an extremity. It is only when all efforts to comprehend the wishes of a conductor have failed that the players accept the responsibility for the performance as their own and, largely speaking, disregard the conductor.

[33]

This does not mean that a conductor must necessarily have what is called a "good stick" or a mastery of any other of the conventional approaches to conducting to qualify for an orchestra's approval. A "good stick"—that is, a well-defined, clearly outlined beat—can certainly be an asset, but it is by no means indispensable from the standpoint of the orchestral player. What is indispensable is the conductor's power to convey sound musicianship, an unaffected sympathy for the music he chooses to conduct.

Georges Enesco, the Roumanian composer and conductor, is a guest welcomed by any orchestra, even though his movements and gestures are an animated contradiction of everything pedagogues of "baton technique" have ever written. He never asks an orchestra to do anything which contradicts the players' feeling of what the music signifies or what the printed notes of the score actually mean in plain musical language. Moreover, as a kind of musicianly virtuoso (both of the violin and piano) and as a composer whose music is unassailably genuine, he has the advantage of an unspoken and an affectionate communication with the men he conducts. To his credit he does not pretend to omniscience. When a certain progression of programs with the Philharmonic decreed that he conduct the Brahms fourth symphony two seasons ago he disavowed intensive rehearsals with the simple statement to the orchestra, "Gentlemen, you know the work better than I do."

Both the compliment and the attitude endeared themselves so much to the orchestra that they literally forgot themselves in a mass effort to justify his statement—and, as one of those who heard the performance, I can testify that they delivered one of the most powerful and integrated interpretations of the score that New York has experienced in seasons.

Another conductor widely admired by musicians is Sir Thomas Beecham, who has unaccountably escaped a mass popularity in this country. With orchestral players his jovial hearty un-neurotic approach to music is as welcome as it is uncommon. It is the contradiction of the mystical approach of the Mengelbergs and Furtwaenglers, embodying, toward the men with whom he works, something of an Empire-attitude. The wide range of his interests—from Mozart to Balakirev and Delius to Purcell—is a testimony not only to his intellectual open-mindedness but also to the happy circumstance that made him the son of a multimillionaire.

Devoid of the success-or-failure frenzy in his approach to music, he addresses himself to conducting with the casual but thoroughgoing enjoyment of an epicure ordering a meal at a very fine restaurant, indifferent to the cost and uninterested in the opinions of those about him. He conducted English music when the most popular English composers were Arthur Sullivan and Handel (an English possession by annexation) and continues to do so today, when the most popular English composers are Reginald Forsyth and Ray Noble. Like most conductors, he fancies himself a wit; but in distinction to all others, his jokes are invariably good.

There are few conductors who impress an orchestra (also composers) at first contact as strongly as does Fritz Reiner, whose knowledge of everything pertaining to the mechanical performance of music is, briefly, unparalleled. He has evolved a personal sign language which leads an orchestra through the most complex scores of Strauss or Stravinsky with the ease and sureness of a tightrope walker who performs a backward somersault blindfolded. Whenever the complexity of the scoring is a sufficient challenge to his skill Reiner will subdivide beats, flash successive cues to remote sections of the orchestra with either hand and meanwhile indicate the pianissimo, in which he takes such great delight, by a bodily movement that totals by a kind of physical mathematics to the exact effect on the printed page. His ear is so acute, not only for intonation but also for dynamics, that he can detect a wrong bowing when his back is turned to the section from which it emanates.

Together with these faculties is a facility for terrifying inferior orchestras unequaled among conductors of the present day. His technique in this sphere is no less sophisticated than it is in his conducting. A mere series of facial expressions can shade his degrees of contempt for a nervous oboist or a fright-palsied violinist as artfully as he fades an orchestra from mezzo piano to pianississimo. His passion for the least audible of possible sounds has created among violinists a new form of occupational ailment known as *Reinerparalysis*. When he is sufficiently challenged by an operatic score, such as *Der Rosenkavalier*, or by the collaboration with a fine soloist, to marshal all his virtuosity, he can achieve fabulous results. The reaction he induces from the orchestras he has conducted runs the full gamut of all emotions but deep affection.

Discussion of this conductor leads one inevitably to Pierre Monteux, who may be described as a more amiable Reiner. An invincible master of the orchestra and everything that pertains to it, he has the experience and knowledge of even the more obscure orchestral instruments which permit him to advise a virtuoso of the bassoon how to better his fingering and breath control for a difficult passage. He is the pedagogue par excellence of orchestral playing, administering his advice in a firm, friendly way that may be classified as a blend of Parisian precision and Munich *gemütlich-keit*.

His service to music as an art and a history has been almost greater than that of any other contemporary conductor, for he performed virtually all of the pre-war "modern" works—including Stravinsky's "Le Sacre du Printemps"—when such sponsorship required as much physical courage as intellectual ability. Even today every conductor who performs the "Sacre" (including Stravinsky) consciously or unconsciously imitates Monteux Orchestral players are invariably ecstatic about his beat, his precision, his clarity, but are vague on his Beethoven and Brahms, saying that they forget how it was. I recall a stunning perform-ance by him of a Handel concerto grosso with the NBC orchestra, while—believe it or not—waiting for him to play "La Valse." One may say of Monteux that he can charm, delight, instruct or cajole orchestral musicians but lacks the aggressiveness to inspire awe.

Awe, however, is the word for Otto Klemperer—known to his intimates as "Doctor" Klemperer. Before I present his qualities as a conductor I would like to lay the unfounded rumor that it was he who introduced Gilbert and Sullivan's works to Düsseldorf. I have a special affection for the good doctor based on his chronological rejection of my compositions with a passionate sincerity that first impressed me immeasurably and then ripened into love. I go for the good doctor. In proportion to his monumental stature is a room-filling voice, an incontrovertible sincerity, a hearty contempt for any humor except the most serious. His prodigious capacity for work, his exuberant vitality and his extraordinary instinct for sponsoring worthwhile new music (during his last season with the Philharmonic he introduced three such outstanding scores as Berg's "Lulu" suite, the Hindemith symphony "Mathis der Maler," and the Janáček symphony) are all bars to his ready acceptance by orchestral players. He demands of musicians the same inexorable, ruthless regime (in attitude, playing and mere platform behavior) that he imposes on himself. As one member of the Philharmonic Symphony expressed himself after a rehearsal, "Two hours with Klemperer is like two hours in church."

The pontifical attitude was a strong factor also in the personality of Walter Damrosch, about whose conducting I have a certain reluctance to speak though I cannot think of any good reason for being reluctant. Perhaps it was because his regime at the head of the New York Symphony contained more than a strong hint of the feudal system. The orchestra was, in fact, virtually a Damrosch possession, founded by father Leopold Damrosch, expiring while a Damrosch still conducted it. It has been more than hinted that Harry Harkness Flagler, who discharged its deficit for many years, would have continued to support it had Damrosch been willing to step aside for some stronger opponent to Toscanini and the Philharmonic. Could it be possible that Damrosch preferred to have the orchestra disbanded rather than to permit its continuance under other direction? In any case, as a sentimental gesture he presented each member of the orchestra with a pair of cuff links at the final concert.

Georges Barrere, the peerless flutist of the orchestra and a brilliant wit, contemplated his gift and remarked sadly, "First he takes the shirt off our backs and then he gives us cuff links."

During his years as an active (the word is comparative) conductor Damrosch sponsored what might be called an inverted virtuosity. Some conductors display their mastery by playing everything faster than it should be, but with Damrosch it took the form of beginning everything slower than anybody else and then getting progressively slower. He reached the zenith of his career against the imposing competition of Josef Stransky, whom a member of his orchestra once threatened with the words, "If you bawl me out again I'll follow your beat."

Musicians may differ in their opinions of the preceding conductors, but of Toscanini, Koussevitzky and Stokowski the orchestras of New York, Boston and Philadelphia have one universal emotion—no matter how intensely they resent the effort these men require of them, they invariably look forward with expectancy to their return. Playing for a lesser, more pleasant man may have its compensations in mental ease and physical relaxation, yet these orchestras are not unlike the married man who welcomes occasional philandering but is nevertheless unhappy except in the familiar, if demanding, routine of his home.

Contrary to the common legend, Koussevitzky does read a score—not very well. Aside from his musical personality, Koussevitzky is altogether more a legend to the outside world than an actuality. Though his is the only non-union orchestra in the country, it is in effect a closed shop so far as the emanation of gossip is concerned. He is unparalleled in the performance of Russian music, whether it is by Moussorgsky, Rimsky-Korsakoff, Strauss, Wagner or Aaron Copland. He is also an enthusiast for Mahler and K. P. E. Bach, which, for a conductor of Russian background, is almost as astonishing as his mastery of the double bass.

Few reports leak out of the Kremlinlike secrecy which surrounds the preparation of his programs, but his players have an internal pride in their status as members of the orchestra—unquestionably the finest in the world—even if they resent the manner in which his miracles are wrought. An inquiry about his rehearsals invariably produces the same enigmatic smile, but no information and less satisfaction.

Over a similar period, however, no conductor in America has produced so many valid new works, both domestic and foreign. It is significant that he has conducted no other orchestra than his own in America, which may be an expression of affection for his own men or a silent criticism of other orchestras. (Or is it because his orchestra is not unionized?) No matter how unpleasant his mannerisms may be in certain classical scores, there is invariably one work on his program so magnificently played that the memory of all others is effaced.

As a surmise, one might guess that Toscanini would find the Koussevitzky treatment of the classics extremely distasteful and artificial, so different is it from his own. Paradoxically, however, the end result is frequently the same. There is the same insistence on purity of sound, blending of choirs, effacement of blemishes and personality of phrasing. Many orchestral players consider Toscanini cruel, inflexible and even petty, citing his inclination to find fault with musicians for no other reason than a dislike of their facial characteristics or the way they sit while playing. One such unfortunate, a violinist, was the invariable target of his criticism because of his mottled complexion. During a visit by the orchestra to another city someone in the violin section made a false entrance, and Toscanini, in a rage, placed the blame squarely on his *bête noire*—even though the musician had remained in New York, ill. I know of no man, however, who does not consider him the greatest conductor, *qua conductor*, with whom he has ever played.

It is an amazing reputation that he has built up on

the basis of a really remarkably small range of interests, which merely underlines his superiority to other
men in most of the works he conducts. Russian music,
save for the Frenchified Ravel version of Moussorgsky's "Pictures from an Exposition," is a closed book
to him; French music, save for certain isolated works
by Ravel and Debussy, is equally outside his ken
(there was evidence of this in the adverse reaction in
the Parisian press to his conducting of "Bolero" and
Dukas's "L'Apprenti Sorcier"); leaving English and
American music, which he rarely conducts, and German and Italian music.

Despite his magnificently vital and invigorating
playing of Beethoven, Wagner, Brahms and Haydn,
it is incontestable that they were recognized as composers of merit before Toscanini "revealed" them and
have a fair chance of survival when he has retired. It is
a fallacy to assume that clarity and the most meticulous
fidelity to a composer's indications are the *open sesame*
to a complete projection of a musical work. Sibelius,
for example, rescored and altered his fifth symphony
three times before arriving at a satisfactory expression
of his purpose. Texture and the most painstaking exposition of it are not necessarily the unfailing road to
the heart of a work. In his sponsorship of this approach

Toscanini, in some circumstances, is inclined to give a composer too much credit.

Musicians are by no means agreed that his Debussy is beyond criticism—the tonal haze that envelopes some of his finest passages is too often denied by Toscanini's all-revealing clarity and tonal balancing. In the same way his Strauss (save for "Tod und Verklärung" and "Don Juan") is often X-rayed rather than recreated, the story-telling element subordinated to his obsession for literal statement.

He has done so little contemporary music that his preferences, except among the Italians, can hardly be discussed. He has sponsored no controversial music of merit in his twelve years as a symphonic conductor in New York, invariably choosing contemporary works for which someone else has done the pioneering. No program of his has ever shown the names of such outstanding contemporaries as Bartok, Hindemith and Schoenberg, and the only Stravinsky he conducts are the "Firebird" and "Petrouchka" suites, each as safe as Mendelssohn's "Calm Sea and Prosperous Voyage." He would have done more for American music had he played none at all, for the works he has played are neither representative nor deserving of such sponsorship. In the one field of contemporary music—the Italian—which he has investigated with any thoroughness, he has avoided the works of the two most adventurous men, Malipiero and Casella, preferring those of the pretty-pretty or "sweeter-than-sweet" school.

Nevertheless, he has every physical and temperamental attribute of the complete conductor, including an indomitable authority, a tenacious and communicative vitality, a brilliant rhythmic sense and an infallible ear. He even possesses the resource of a burning wit, as may be testified by his imperious remark to a violinist who spent every slight pause in a rehearsal tuning his instrument: "It's not the A that counts, but the B." Despite the captious comments above, Toscanini remains the "infallible conductor."

I have also the recollection of a conductor—prominent in the days before the animated cartoon reached its zenith—who was the veritable enchantress of the orchestral world. (I use the feminine gender aesthetically.) I miss the tumult he created both with the orchestra and the press. Physically he had a considerable resemblance to the contemporary Hollywood figure known as Leopold Stokowski, but the latter is obviously an impostor, taking advantage of this resemblance. A musical Lawrence of Arabia, one scarcely knew from whence the authentic Stokowski came or what his background (prior to the Cincinnati Symphony days) was. Suddenly he emerged in full flower, bringing to orchestral conducting a quality which personalized it almost as completely as Dhiagileff did the Russian Ballet. Essentially, he had tremendous merit as a creative conductor, not alone in his treatment of music but also in his approach to the mere physical properties of conducting.

I would like to have been present, if I could have my choice of all moments in musical history, when Stokowski suddenly became conscious of his beautiful hands. *That* must have been a moment. Like stout Cortez on a peak in Darien (I know it was Balboa) he saw before him a limitless expanse, a whole uncharted sea that might be subjected to his influence, free from the encumbrance of a baton.

Then came the period of conducting "Scheherazade" from behind a screen, while the mystic shapes of the Color Organ played on it; of reseating the cellos (a musical adaptation of the Notre Dame shift, Knute Rockne then being prominent) to his right; of doing away with the lights on the stage because they distracted the audience, and then beaming an overhead spotlight directly on his tawny mane as he conducted;

of the Javanese gongs, the Indian Temple Bells, the Chinese scales; of lecturing his audiences for not applauding a modern work, though it was not clear whether the lecture was based on a sincere admiration for the composer or on an unslakable lust for publicity.

As a gesture to abolish class distinctions in the first violin section he did away with the institution of concertmaster, thereby creating sixteen prima donnas in place of the one he had before. Nevertheless, when he allowed each of them to bow as they might, without regard for the tradition of uniformity observed by virtually all other orchestras, the results, for him and the audience, were excellent. In a later period came the passion for arranging, for making gorgeous tone poems out of Bach's organ pieces, of a Palestrina chorus, of a Buxtehude toccata. But the incomparably polished and iridescent playing of the orchestra—as slick, colorful and vibrant as the audience it attracted—virtually put Bach, for the first time, on the Hit Parade. It is quite possible that if he had not become sated with music (and success) he eventually would have conducted the orchestra blindfolded, with his left arm tied behind his back.

He created, in the Philadelphia Orchestra of the

mid-twenties, an instrument that demonstrated in its exquisitely sensual sound, its urbane virtuosity, how well a hundred men could be made to play together. But, possibly surfeited with this accomplishment, he became the dandy of orchestral conductors, a veritable musical Lucius Beebe, wearing his scores like so many changes of attire.

There finally came the period when his vagaries were infinitely more exciting and arousing than the correct traditionalism of the lesser "scholarly" conductors. But when his vagaries became successful—no doubt to his subconscious disgust—he found himself at an impasse. They had germinated the embryo of a new tradition with which—because it had become fixed and static—he was no longer in sympathy. This left him an unwritten character out of Huxley's *Point Counter Point*, with his original ennui. The only vagary left to him was to give up conducting.

At this moment, however, his return to the Philadelphia Orchestra is certain, for which I am fervently grateful. This certainty may be contradicted by the last minute arrival of a fascinating script, however.

There are a million lights in a million Philadelphia windows for him.

Hurry home, Leo, all is forgiven.

Memoirs Of a Mute

Memoirs Of a Mute

FOR MORE THAN FIFTEEN YEARS THE
first person that almost every visiting celebrity to
Hollywood expressed a desire to meet was Charlie
Chaplin; inevitably in second place was Harpo Marx.
Recently Harpo has been moving ahead in the great
Celebrity Sweepstakes, until now the chances are
even that as many will ask to meet Harpo as Chaplin.
I should not be surprised, indeed, if the lead passes
definitely to Marx before the year is out, although
Harpo is quite content with his position as runner-up,

[53]

deferring to the matchless artistry of his predecessor in pantomime.

That the two most celebrated silent men of the now articulate films exercise an irresistible fascination for some of the greatest conversationalists of our time is more than mildly curious. One can only conclude that there must be some subconscious attraction in their silence. Naturally, also, everyone wonders what a man who never says anything sounds like.

Though Harpo is one of the most ill-informed men I have ever encountered, it was as a consequence of his fascination for savants and celebrities that I had the pleasure of meeting some of the day's most distinguished citizens at his home in Hollywood. One could never be sure in accepting a dinner invitation to Harpo's whether one's companions would be H. G. Wells and Don Budge, or Somerset Maugham and Salvador Dali. Frequently the combinations were even more remarkable—Aldous Huxley and Maxie Rosenbloom.

Despite these efforts to live up to Woollcotts' ecstatic characterization of him as an incurable zany (a well-meaning but misguided bit of propaganda which, I am sure, has taxed Harpo's ingenuity now for all of ten years) he is in reality a person of complete conventionality—as Howard Dietz said, "the most normal person I know."

From everything that occurred between us, I would say that Harpo found me a rather amusing person, though he was sometimes shocked by what he considered to be my bad manners. (It was not uncommon for this most celebrated madman to introduce me half-apologetically to a friend as if to prepare him for some outrageous insanity.)

I found him a man generous with money, rather un-exciting and a wonderful audience. His qualities were best epitomized on the occasion that I met George S. Kaufman in New York and asked if he had heard recently from Harpo.

"How," he asked, "how can you hear from Harpo? He can't write and he can't talk, so how can you hear from Harpo?"

I first met Harpo at a Gershwin concert at the Stadium in New York eight or nine years ago. He had no ticket and was trying (unsuccessfully) to work his way in through the back gate when I came up with an extra ticket and offered it to him. However, it is now Harpo's story that we had met in some obscure way previously, that I was lonely that night and called him up, begging him to come with me. Further, he contends that he had a date, but that I begged so hard he finally consented to go just to keep me company.

Through our mutual friends, the Gershwins, Irving Berlin, Kaufman, Moss Hart and others, I saw him quite frequently after that, particularly while he was working in New York in various shows. (Somehow, though, I never did get around to seeing any show in which the Marxes appeared.) Sometime after this we went to Woollcott's place in Vermont for a week end together with another mutual friend, Charlie Lederer. We prepared ourselves for the trip and the week end by buying seven "Tarzan" books and two quarts of ice cream before getting on the train.

We had barely pulled out of the station when Harpo, after a short tour of exploration, returned with the information that there was a stunning girl in lower 7. Summoning the porter, we dispatched a message suggesting that she join us for a spot of ice cream. In a moment he returned, followed by a veritable gargoyle. It was by this time too late to rescind the invitation, but while she consumed a full quart of ice cream Harpo quietly disappeared, his tasty little joke consummated.

On another occasion we were driving on Long Island when Harpo spied ahead of us an ancient Baker electric, piloted by two prim dowagers. He drew abreast of them and with his most oafish facial expression leaned from the car, pointed a finger in a generally westerly direction and inquired, "Denver?"

Several weeks later we again went to Long Island, this time to visit Herbert Bayard Swope. (I hope the Swopes do not take offense at this. It's about the only house I have left.) Harpo was accompanied by his man of all work, valet, secretary and trainer, who also drove his car. As Harpo hardly felt that he had attained the dignity of a uniformed chauffeur, his man wore no livery. Moreover, he was an amiable chap who was not above strolling about the grounds and mingling with the guests, watching a game of tennis or whatever interested him. Eventually he came upon Swope, who was engaged in croquet with a group of experts. With his training in public life, Swope prides himself on his ability to remember not only a face, but the name that goes with it, after a single meeting. (His talent in this sphere is said to compare favorably with Jim Farley's.)

When the stranger joined the group, Swope looked at him closely and resumed his play. The shot completed, he glanced up again, more intently this time. Plainly he was searching his mind to recall the identity of this onlooker. Finally confessing defeat, he strode up to the young man, extended his hand and said in his heartiest presidential-timbre manner,

"Good afternoon. I'm Herbert Bayard Swope."

"Pleased to meet'cha," he responded. "I'm Benny Murphy, Harpo's chauffeur."

One of Harpo's distinguishing traits is his fondness for receiving guests in the nude, playing the harp in a pair of shorts. Deeply immersed in a Bach "Bourée" or his *pièce de resistance* "Mighty Lak' A Rose," with an interminable cadenza, he will greet them blandly, calmly indifferent to their shocked surprise. His pretense of having forgotten the invitation is a beautiful thing to see.

I had a personal experience with that humor several years ago when Harpo, along with the other Marxes, settled permanently to work and live in Hollywood. He had taken quite a large house in Beverly Hills, where there was living with him at the time S. N. Behrman, the playwright, and Max Gordon, the producer. Nightly when I returned from doing a broadcast in New York I would find wires from Harpo, urging me to come out and spend a few months in Hollywood. He even offered to pay half my fare, and I replied, that was fine, I'd go to Kansas City.

However, as I was playing piano on five radio shows at the time I had good reason for staying in New York. But Harpo's wires became more tantalizing, and I finally picked a fight at the studio—the jobs bored me though I liked the money—and quit.

This accomplished, I sent a wire to Harpo saying, "Have you room for me?"

He wired back, "Come, but have no room."

Naturally I was furious and poured out my resentment at this treatment in a wire to Behrman. He answered promptly, saying, "Come, will take care of you."

In sequence came a telegram from Harpo, saying, "I love you, but I can't live in the same house with you."

The matter reached a climax when Behrman sent a mollifying message to me, and I responded that I would accept *his* invitation, but not Harpo's. When I arrived I refused to acknowledge Harpo's greeting or talk to him. I did, however, have a hearty dinner; and for the next four months I had lunch, dinner and supper at Harpo's, without exchanging a word with him. I would, of course, talk with any of the sixteen other persons that invariably sat down to dinner at his table, but never with Harpo.

It was not strange, therefore, that I eventually developed the feeling that Behrman and I owned the place, and that we were merely tolerating Harpo. One night I invited a guest of my own to dinner, at which even Harpo was a little startled. As we sat down at the table Behrman said to me (in the hearing of everyone at the table, including Harpo),

"Why don't you speak to Harpo?"

"The hell with that," I responded. "I'm sore at him."

"But after all," said Behrman, "he's your host."

"No," I answered stubbornly, "he isn't."

"Who is your host?" queried Behrman, puzzled. "And who is the host of your friend who comes as your guest, but you have no host?"

With this Behrman embarked on a flood of casuistry, intoxicated by the rhythm of his words. Rocking and rolling like a Talmudic scholar feasting on an insoluble problem, he continued, "You've been eating three meals a day here for four months, and now you even bring a guest. Then you deny that Harpo is your host. This is taking on the clear, unanswerable obscurity of a Pirandello play."

After I had been at Pension Marx for upward of four months thoughts of returning to New York City naturally identified themselves with the hope of a job —possibly with the producer who was the honored guest one night at dinner. We had scarcely disposed of the entrée when Harpo turned to this producer, remarking in a loud, clear voice which no one at the table could ignore, "Oscar says you have no talent." With that, he quietly resumed his dinner.

This was embarrassing to me, even though I do not embarrass easily, and I said,

"Harpo, that's a dirty trick."

Baffled, and not quite sure what to say, the producer attempted to relieve the tension by saying,

"What's the difference as long as I'm a nice fellow?"

To this, Charlie Lederer interposed helpfully,

"That's a moot point."

Harpo, perhaps, valued the presence of his literary guests because their talk acted as a powerful soporific upon him. I have rarely seen the equal of the mellow, easeful mood that would descend on Harpo after an hour or two at the dinner table. He would be utterly charming to his guests until the inevitable reaction set in. Then he would politely excuse himself and go upstairs to bed.

One of the most enjoyable evenings I had at Harpo's found Maxie Rosenbloom as the lion. Maxie, the celebrated comedian and ex-light-heavyweight boxing champion, was in a perpetual state of retirement, but he would just as soon fight as act. In any case, his past in the ring was still very much with him. On this occasion a fascinating portion of his recitation was devoted to his brother, also a boxer, who had too much pride to trade on the family name of Rosenbloom. Consequently he adopted the *nom de ring* of Sinclair Walsh.

Of his own career, Maxie was most voluble about the portion of his skill which won him the title of "Slapsie-Maxie"—his phenomenal skill as a boxer and particularly his deftness in handling the open glove. In consequence he had built up a remarkable reputation as a boxer and was inordinately proud of the fact that he never resorted to such crude tactics as a knockout to achieve his victories and, indeed, rarely knocked a man down. Thus he was righteously indignant at an episode that happened during a bout in Colorado when he was giving an exhibition of his specialty, dancing about and pecking away with ineffable grace. One of his open gloves made a contact with his dazzled opponent, who promptly collapsed on the canvas.

Enraged, Maxie looked down at him and bellowed, "Why you dirty double-crossing rat!"

Apropos of prize fighters, I must not omit the saga

of the Marxes in their adventures as prize-fighter managers. In some obscure way they had acquired the services of a heavyweight fighter, whom they promptly named "Canvasback." I do not contend that the designation was unjustified, for I had seen "Canvasback" in what might laughingly be called action; but it was always my feeling that the name did not do much to build up his confidence. However, the peak of their enterprise was accomplished on an evening when "Canvasback" exceeded his ordinary quota by being knocked down five times in the first round. As he tottered to his corner Groucho and Harpo leaped into the ring, prepared to exert their skill in readying him for the next round. As he sat down, however, Harpo shoved "Canvasback" brusquely to the floor while Groucho proceeded to fan his brother energetically!

On the occasion of H. G. Wells's visit to the house I was somewhat nettled that he devoted all of his fascinated attention to Harpo. I, who had read virtually all of Wells's output, was a much better conversationalist than Harpo (as modest a statement as I can think of)—and I might as well have not been in the room for all the attention Wells paid to me!

I had a much better time when Harpo had Aldous Huxley as his dinner guest. For one thing, there was his thorough knowledge of music and his great sensitivity to it as a bond between us. He was present in Hollywood as a consultant, because of his excellent scientific equipment, on the script of "Mme Curie," to which Greta Garbo had been assigned. Many elaborate preparations were being taken to insure the scientific accuracy of the script, resulting in innumerable story conferences. At one of them the discussion turned to the nature of Mme Curie's scientific accomplishments, and Huxley launched into a fascinating exposition of atomic structure, the function of the molecule and other related subjects.

This was not merely an authoritative statement of the whole atmosphere in which the film was immersed, but also a brilliant monologue, embellished by all of Huxley's subtle feeling for words, his exceptional skill in narration. As he approached the climax of his excellently logical discourse someone interrupted querulously,

"Come, come. What's the story point?"

Perhaps that is why "Mme Curie" was never produced, with Garbo or without her.

As a lesser example of Harpo's hospitality I should mention the evening when, impressed by my stories of Arnold Schoenberg's eminence as a composer and his fine personal qualities, Harpo invited him as the honored guest at a ceremonial dinner. As the proper complement to Schoenberg—or perhaps in utter innocence of any consequences—the eminent composer and myself were greeted when we arrived together by two of Harpo's friends who happened to be in Hollywood at the time—Beatrice Lillie and Fannie Brice.

Schoenberg had only the haziest idea who Lillie and Brice were, while they were altogether mystified by him. To make conversation, Brice inquired what "hits" Schoenberg had written; and after dinner she kept coaxing Schoenberg with, "C'mon, professor, play us a tune." I never found out whether she expected him to provide her with a successor to "My Man" or possibly a comedy song like "I'm an Indian."

Regardless of whether a visitor to the coast was a cabinet member, a banker or the dean of a university, he rarely appeared in Hollywood without a letter of introduction to Harpo. In due course he would make his way to the Marx dinner table where Harpo presided over his cluster of disciples like a mute Socrates.

Only on one occasion did we encounter someone who could euphemistically be described as our match. This was the youthful Randolph Churchill, son of England's First Lord of the Admiralty, Winston

Churchill. He came with the reputation of being even more than a London equivalent of me—the most bumptious, loudmouthed, impertinent person that English society has produced in our generation. At dinner he succeeded in insulting everybody at the table before the main course had arrived. It was at the time when Landon was contesting Roosevelt's right to a second term in the White House, and Churchill argued vehemently for the merits of the Republican, as if the election had not already been decided two days before. Since one of Harpo's most treasured possessions is an inscribed photograph of the President, it may be understood how popular this made Churchill with his host.

After dinner we attempted to exact retribution by taking Churchill to a ping-pong parlor and imposing on him the labor of retrieving the balls, which, mysteriously, were being batted consistently to the most inaccessible corners of the room. This did not faze him, however, nor did it diminish his capacity for the querulous.

News of his behavior at Harpo's filtered back to New York, and especially to Swope, whose letter of introduction had effected his invitation to Harpo's. In the morning Churchill received a wire:

"Don't forget you're not only representing the Empire. You're also representing Swope."

Despite this admonition Churchill was hardly chastened when we invited him on the following evening to one of my favorite Hollywood houses—Salka Viertel's. Salka, I should point out, is Garbo's personal representative and wife of Berthold Viertel, the celebrated poet and director. As an old Berliner, she automatically had become the social arbiter in California for the many refugees, both German and Austrian, in Hollywood—such as Korngold, Schoenberg, Toch, Klemperer and Reinhardt. Her house was the gathering place for all of these, comprising what I called the "fast-drinking Schwartzwald set."

With scarcely any important exception the wives of all of these, and most of the other guests that one was likely to encounter there, were ex-Reinhardt actresses, in consequence of which all valuations were couched in terms of Greek drama.

"What was she like as a young girl?" I once heard Salka ask, in discussing the youth of a mutual female friend.

"A rather poor Klytemnestra," replied her informant.

Mrs Klemperer, too, was hardly more proud of her

husband than she was of the fact that in her youth she had been "a fine Medea." Salka herself once reported that she had won the "most-beautiful-legs contest in Vienna" before embarking on her studies with Professor Reinhardt. She had her first quarrel with him shortly after that when she insisted on playing Lady Macbeth.

It was into this atmosphere, redolent of the theater, that Churchill was projected on the occasion of his visit with us. Actually, the torch of the drama was burning with particular brightness that night, heightened by the reflected glow from Ernst Lubitsch, the evening's particular lion. The air was thick with talk of parts, roles, great performances, the mystery of the footlights and so on, when Salka turned to our companion and said,

"And you, Mr Churchill, do you like the theater?"

Economically, almost aggressively, he answered, "No!"

In the audible silence that descended on the room Salka found voice to inquire,

"Why?"

"Because," said Churchill, "you can't smoke in the theater."

Despite the egregious impudence of this young man,

whom Heywood Broun immortalized as "England's ambassador of ill-will," I confess that I had a fondness for his breezy impertinence, his indifference to anything describable as public opinion—and also for his really sharp intelligence.

On the day following his triumph at the Viertels' he was scheduled to receive the press at the Brown Derby during lunch, and I accompanied him. It was November, but an exceedingly warm day which made me uncomfortable in my vestless suit. Churchill, however, turned up in an imposing fur-lined greatcoat, giving him all the aura of statesmanship.

He handled himself well with the newspapermen, even if he did seem a little insensitive to the satire of one young reporter who kept referring to him constantly as the "future Prime Minister." Churchill accepted the nomination placidly, even appearing indifferent to the fact that his one sortie into politics as a candidate for Parliament resulted in his defeat, as he himself phrased it, by "the largest majority in English governmental history."

I was abundantly impressed, too, by the lunch he had on this day. Despite the hour and the heat of the day he began with mushrooms under glass, followed by shrimp, as preliminaries to a double order of pork chops with extra potatoes, leading to salad, an impressive dessert and, of course, the usual cheese and coffee. Virtually a whole meal served Under Bell.

When I expressed my wonder at this and asked him how he did it Churchill responded airily,

"Americans just pick at food. I like to eat heartily."

As a final touch in his campaign of ingratiating himself with the film colony came Churchill's encounter with Jack Warner of Warner Brothers. It was then that he established his true claim to be described as the "irrepressible Churchill." Warner was holding forth on some subtle point incident to the intricate art of producing, not without difficulty, owing to the incessant interruptions of Churchill, who was full of suggestions for improving Warner Brothers' output.

Finally, in exasperation with Churchill's eighth interruption, Warner turned to him and said heatedly,

"Young man, when you're my age——"

"You'll be eighty," interjected Churchill blithely.

It would be a gross injustice for me to leave this phase of Harpo and Hollywood without a further documentation of Salka and her set. Hers was a house in which there was an endless chess tournament always in progress. When Schoenberg came he arrived literally with his own ping-pong racquets. As for conversation, the theater was only a preliminary to literature, painting, sculpture and music. One of the most heated arguments between two women which it has ever been my uneasy experience to overhear occurred one evening when one argued violently, and the other dissented as vigorously, as to whether Schoenberg's eyes did or did not dance.

Hovering constantly in the background was the pianist Eduard Steuermann, the celebrated interpreter of very new and very old music and, incidentally, Salka's brother. His favorite repertory piece, on these occasions, was the Goldberg variations of Bach, which he would play on the drop of a hint or with none at all. Sometimes, as an apéritif, he would serve Reger's scarcely succinct variations on a theme by Bach.

My favorite comment on his playing was offered by Erich Korngold, a staunch supporter of this circle, who saluted the end of a Steuermann recital with the words,

"He plays good—no?"

Following this Korngold took his place at the piano to play some music of his own. I remember in particular a waltz which Korngold played so lustily and with such enthusiasm, with a manner truly *Wiener-*

isch, that the ivory (somewhat loosened by the Santa Monica sea air) began to peel from the keys. Unperturbed, Korngold brushed them away and continued to play as though it were an everyday occurrence for the ivory to come off the keys when he played. It was authoritatively reported that all of Santa Monica reeled under the impact of his bass, and the seismograph at U.C.L.A. registered a major tremor.

When he had finished I took my turn at the piano and played some snatches of the Gershwin concerto which he had not heard previously. Korngold was hardly eager to be enthusiastic about this, but he could not conceal some slight pleasure with the finale. After this he asked for "The Man I Love" and, in sequence, Vincent Youmans' "Tea for Two." Then he turned triumphantly and said, "See—a note for note steal." This was incomprehensible to me and still is today, as I recall it, for even the slightest resemblance does not exist between the two songs—in mood, melodic line or harmony.

With this circle in mind, I composed a mock French opera called *Le Crayon est sur la table*, utilizing all the Debussy clichés from "Pelleas"—the descending fourth in the voice parts, the parallel seventh chords and the interrogatory "Pourquoi?" The text ran the full range of my Berlitz-school French and was grammatical if nothing else. I would play and sing it incessantly for an hour at a time, setting all the Germans crazy. The news of this got around in Hollywood, and the 20th Century-Fox trade paper (I was then employed at that studio) reported in all seriousness, "Our staff composer Oscar Levant is working on an opera called *Le Crayon est sur la table*."

During all this time I was studying with Schoenberg, and with my piano concerto completed, I was anxious to have it performed. Schoenberg offered to intercede with Klemperer on my behalf, and for a little time after that I heard nothing further. However, one night at Salka's in the midst of an uncommonly noisy and talkative gathering Klemperer came over and said he would like to hear some of my concerto. Not considering this the proper atmosphere for an event so important to me, I sat down at the piano, and with Charlie Lederer providing a lusty tenor, performed "When Irish Eyes are Smiling," the last sixteen measures of "My Hero" (from *The Chocolate Soldier*), with its excruciating ascending climax. We topped it off with a four-hand version of "Chopsticks." Before we reached this finale, however, Klemperer had stalked from the room, with that manner of carrying the podium with him.

[73]

Looking about in search of justification for my boorishness, I asked Schoenberg,

"Dr Klemperer is angry?"

"Worse," said Schoenberg. "He is bored."

For six months after this whenever I called Klemperer's home in an effort to conciliate the situation I was informed, "Dr Klemperer is taking a walk in the garden."

Not only the monotony of the answer but also its uninventiveness offended me. However, I finally restored myself to his good graces by calling on him, together with Jerome Moross, in the green room after a fine concert he directed with the Los Angeles Philharmonic. Perhaps his geniality to me was in part conditioned by the success of the concert, at which Nathan Milstein played the Mendelssohn violin concerto; or perhaps by Klemperer's pleasure in the work. (I recall that he was voluble in his praise of Mendelssohn's orchestration, as if experiencing it for the first time.) In any case he agreed to examine the scores of my piano concerto and orchestral nocturne.

When he had completed his study of the scores I went to see him. He looked at me severely and said, "You are undoubtedly very talented."

I recognized this as the kiss of death and replied,

"That means you are not going to play my music."

In surprise Klemperer asked, "How did you know?"

"For years now," I answered, "whenever anybody turns me down they tell me how talented I am. If a man is going to hire me he says, 'Come in Monday morning at nine o'clock.' If a conductor is going to play a piece of music the first thing he asks for is 'a few changes here and there.' But if it's thumbs down I always am praised for my talent."

Klemperer saw I was vexed and said consolingly, "What's your hurry? Bruckner was fifty before his first symphony was played." He also advised me to play the Beethoven piano sonatas every morning.

There were, of course, other houses in Hollywood where music was not only tolerated but encouraged, not the least of them Harpo's. As possibly the only prominent movie performer—aside from singers—to be identified with music, Harpo was naturally a figure of some prominence in Hollywood's musical life. Actually, when Leopold Stokowski first appeared in Hollywood and was asked by his host to signify a choice of dinner guests he specified Harpo and Irving Berlin. It was possibly merely a coincidence that neither of the eminent music men he invited can read music.

As an intellectual fourth in this tournament of confusion, I was present as a sort of enharmonic modulation between the world of popular music inhabited by Harpo and Berlin and concert music represented by Stokowski. Whether with or without malicious intent, Berlin remarked to Stokowski, as an ice-breaker, "I saw you in *100 Men and A Girl*, and I thought your hands were beautiful."

Stokowski accepted this compliment with appropriate modesty. After some amiable conversation with Berlin about mutual friends, Stokowski turned to Harpo.

"How do you tune your harp?"

"Backward," replied Harpo.

Stokowski recoiled in frigid disdain, fearful that he was being ribbed. Factually, however, Harpo spoke with utter truth. He does tune his harp backward, for that is the way he learned the instrument—wholly by ear—and that is the way he still plays because it is easiest for him. I might point out the further similarity here between Harpo and Chaplin. Not only are they two remarkable silent comics who attract, as I have mentioned before, the great of the earth to their board, but they are both men of musical accomplishment. To complete the interesting parallel is the fact that Chaplin's violin, like Harpo's Lyon and Healy, cannot be played by anyone, but its owner (save perhaps Rudy Kolisch) for Chaplin is left-handed, and the strings are arranged in reverse order—the G string where the E ordinarily is and so on across.

Harpo still absorbs all the additions to his repertory by ear.

He has a particular fondness for Bach, influenced somewhat by the fact that he learns almost all his music by listening to the records of Andreas Segovia, the great Spanish guitarist. Since Segovia plays very little but Bach and Castilian music it is understandable that Harpo's gamut is similarly from B to C.

It came to Harpo's attention while I was enjoying his cuisine that Maurice Ravel had written a work for harp and chamber ensemble, his "Introduction and Allegro." It immediately became a point of pride with Harpo to learn this work, and I was pressed into service as coach and pedagogue, teaching him the work note by note from the piano. As a climax of six months' labor Harpo mastered his part sufficiently to undertake it at one of his soirées. I was present not only to supply a friendly encouraging atmosphere but also to play the instrumental background on the piano, with its integrated solo and ensemble passages.

The performance went very well except that Harpo

at the first opportunity launched into his solo part and played it through without pause, completely ignoring the numerous tuttis that were to be filled in by me at the piano.

Harpo also had certain pretensions as a composer, which I attempted to foster by increasing his knowledge of harmony. Previously the only effects he had been able to manage were those he had learned by ear. However, after six months of instruction (the same six months in which Harpo was learning the Ravel piece) all I was able to teach him was some of those celeste chords that Strauss uses at the beginning of *Rosenkavalier*. With or without these—I can't recall which—Harpo wrote two pieces, which he delights to play under all possible circumstances: one called "Elmer" and the other "Aphrodisiac." It is as the composer of "Elmer" and "Aphrodisiac" that I think most fondly of Harpo.

Among the musical guests to be encountered at Harpo's, I remember with particular vividness Mischa Elman. He was in town on a concert tour and naturally found his way to Harpo's. We went to see *Reunion in Vienna* after dinner, and the treatment of the Hapsburgs distressed Elman considerably. He recounted his experience in playing before the old

[78]

Emperor Franz Josef and said they were not that sort of people. When it was pointed out to him that medical records show that the Hapsburgs were an epileptic family he responded,

"If they were epileptic, then why didn't they throw fits in the picture?"

After the show we went back to the house against a running commentary of Elman experiences in playing before royalty. His most distressing moment, it seems, occurred when he received a royal command to play for George and Mary of England at Windsor Castle. He was engaged in some profound labor, involving much playing on the E string, when two royal dogs, property of the King, loped into the room and took a position beside their master. Each time Elman rose to eloquence on the E string the dogs bayed uncomfortably. Finally after several disregarded blasphemous looks he paused and looked significantly at the dogs with an "either-the-dogs-or-me" expression. However, nobody made a move to remove the dogs, so Elman had to continue the recital with the two dogs dissenting.

Present at Harpo's during the Elman evening was an eminent movie producer, who listened to a critical dissection of several of his recent pictures with considerable tolerance. When everyone had had his say the producer launched into a long defense of his activities, outlining the problems involved in their production, the vast sums of money that had been spent on authenticating details, the stupidity of his actors and the erratic performances of his script writers. He had scarcely paused for breath when Elman inquired mildly,

"If it's so hard to make bad pictures, why don't you make good ones?"

However, the choice Elmanism of that occasion happened out of my hearing. One of the feminine guests of the evening (who had similarly probed the psyches of Kreisler and Heifetz) asked Mischa,

"How does it feel to be Mischa Elman?"

He paused, reflected for a moment and then said (according to her story), "Sometimes I think it's all a dream."

With George Gershwin, I was present one evening when Harpo's guests included the producer of a picture in which the fifth symphony of Tschaikowsky was utilized as an opera. The producer was inordinately proud of this accomplishment, even after I pointed out that each of the characters in the "opera" entered on repetitions of the same motive. The producer regarded this as the establishment of a new trend in musical pictures.

Not without malice, I remarked, "I understand Universal has taken an option of Dvořák's 'New World' symphony."

Taking a paper and pencil from his pocket, he hastily jotted a note, saying, "Thanks for the tip. I'll have to outbid them."

Among Harpo's musical manifestations, not the least was his passion for playing on any stringed instrument, regardless of whether it was guitar, mandolin or banjo. Not infrequently I accompanied him into the remote outskirts of Los Angeles to hear some obscure virtuoso of the frets, and on one occasion he drove me almost to Mexico in search of a superb performer of whom he had been told. He was also a great admirer of Iturbi, whose playing of Mozart with Toscanini had been a cherished memory of a visit to New York. Harpo always went to hear him in Los Angeles with the Philharmonic, and in Hollywood at the Bowl, where he played nothing but Liszt. This rather baffled Harpo.

Though he read less than any man I know, he had a passion for first editions, especially an inscribed Shaw, an early Somerset Maugham ("Liza of Lambeth," as in walk), and a fine Wells, all three of them extremely valuable. Not even in the British Museum could Harpo's "firsts" have been better preserved than they were on the reading table beside his bed, where he liked to look at them before he retired at night. From time to time I would pass by the door casually and glance at the table to see if the books had changed, but no—the same ones were always there in the same place.

As well as being possessed of one of the most amiable, sweet dispositions I have ever encountered in a man, Harpo was an apostle of generosity. Finding myself short of cash one day, I proposed a loan to him, and he escorted me upstairs to his bathroom (which occupied a total floor space equivalent to that of the Roxy lobby) and opened a small safe beside the shower, from which he extracted, in cash, the $200 I needed. It was always my theory that he kept the first editions there during the day, taking them out at night when his guests came.

There was also a period in which he went in for painting, specializing in nudes. When he first started his career he called an agency for a model but failed to specify the particular type he wanted. When the girl appeared he asked her to strip, which she refused to do. So, instead, Harpo stripped to shorts, and painted her as she donned a smock.

From some unrevealed source he had picked up the name of Cgolsz, the madman who assassinated President McKinley. He made quite a bit of money on this, inveigling friends into a discussion of political assassinations and then wagering that he could supply the assassin's name. He was also greatly fascinated by a story I read to him one day from a Los Angeles newspaper. It was during that period several years ago when Polish athletes who had competed in the Olympics as females were suddenly reappearing as males and vice versa. This story concerned a Polish peasant named Nachman who suddenly, and for no explicable reason (after thirty respectable years as a male) gave birth to a daughter. For weeks after that Harpo would announce himself at a friend's house by pounding loudly on the door and proclaiming, "Nachman is here!"

Perhaps the most remarkable experience I ever had with Harpo followed a studio party at which I encountered a charming young girl, who, it developed, was a highly respected member of Los Angeles society. I pressed her for a date, but she replied that it was out of the question until I had presented myself at her house, met her mother and brought along some member of my family. Accordingly I arranged to call a few evenings later at her home, duly appearing with Harpo, whom I presented as my uncle. We were both on the street five minutes later, after Harpo had insulted the butler, chucked the maid under the chin and chased the girl's mother halfway around the house.

His passion for health is pursued with unremitting zeal, involving arduous tennis, gymnastics, intensive sun-bathing, etc. His sleep is singularly untroubled by dreams, and, indeed, he has a capacity for sleep that I have frequently envied. On that early trip to Vermont our sleeper was buffeted about in Albany between two engines for what seemed to me an eternity. (I was as usual in an upper berth.) Harpo had no recollection of the incident on the following morning and, indeed, boasted of the restful night he had spent. On another occasion, during an airplane trip to the coast, he fell asleep during an incredible passage over the Rockies while I contemplated recourse to a parachute. In a dentist's chair he has even been known to doze quietly while his teeth are being drilled.

It was Harpo, too, who accomplished the prodigious feat of falling asleep in a car on the way to his wedding, with his bride-to-be beside him. But psychologically his sleep symbolized security in his marriage, which has been a happy one. Harpo and Susan subsequently adopted a baby, which elicited a wire from me: "Congratulations on your son. If he needs brother wire terms." And that reminds me that, as a youth, Harpo was a boy soprano in a quartet. When he fortunately lost his voice he found that silence was golden.

A Cog In The Wheel

A Cog In The Wheel

IT IS A TRADITION IN PICTURES (ONE OF the most stubbornly respected) that nobody in the world goes to hear a movie score but the composer, the orchestrator and other composers. As a kind of compensation, I suppose, they hear every single sixteenth note in the score and are thereafter equipped to discuss its most obscure subtleties. Frequently, however, they have to be told what the picture itself is about.

This has its parallel in another tradition in the

movies with which every composer comes into contact as soon as he reports to a studio. It was probably devised by the first producer ever to use a musical score for a dramatic film and runs as follows: If the audience doesn't notice the music it's a good score. This I never could quite understand. I have heard many approving, even admiring comments—not all by composers—on scores for foreign pictures written by Auric, Honegger, Shostakovitch, Prokofieff, Francaix and others. Certainly an audience would not find such contributions out of place in an American picture merely because the characters spoke English rather than French, German or Russian.

Perhaps one of the reasons for the low repute of picture music may be found in the words that fill the air when a Hollywood score is discussed by those versed in such matters. You never hear any discussion of a score as a whole. Instead, the references are to "main-title" music, "end title" music, "montages," "inserts" and so on, with no recognition of the character of the complete score. It is much as if one would discuss a suit in terms of its buttonholes, pleats, basting and lining, without once considering its suitability to the figure it adorned.

Even so, this represents a considerable advance in

the liberty formerly permitted movie composers. It is only within the last half-dozen years that a composer for the movies has been allowed to write anything other than a fanfare at the beginning and end of a picture. In the early days of the talkies the idea of writing music under dialogue was so revolutionary that a number of prominent producers (as, for example, Irving Thalberg) countenanced it only under the greatest pressure, and then but sparingly. They were not merely unfriendly to music; they were actually suspicious of its potentialities.

They made a great fetish, for example, of pointing out the conflict between the so-called "reality" of the movies and the "unreality" of music. Always when a situation seemed to demand a heightening by musical effect they would come back at the composer with the question, "But where would the audience think the orchestra is coming from?" This was supposed to be the stopper for all arguments. When a musical background was absolutely inseparable from an effect they would go to the most extravagant lengths to relate the music to the scene by having a band playing outside the window, or secreting a string quartet behind a row of potted palms or having the sound come out of a radio. Unquestionably it is an additional virtue to make music an integral part of a dramatic situation; but it always seemed to me an example of remarkable shortsightedness that even the best directors and producers could not reconcile themselves to the thought that they were dealing with a completely artificial medium and adapt themselves to it accordingly.

I might mention that one of the few early talkies I remember was the movie version of Barry's *Paris Bound*. My memory of its details is extremely hazy, but I do recall with some clarity a musical score for it by Arthur Alexander. In fact that is the only detail that I do recall eight or nine years after it appeared. The only reason that Alexander had the opportunity to write that score was that a ballet figured in the action, and it is customary, after all, for ballets to have music. In addition, the main character is a composer.

What was particularly preposterous about the producers' attitude was that music has been an accepted accessory of the legitimate theater for generations. I seem to recall, even, that Beethoven wrote incidental music for *Egmont*, Mendelssohn for *A Midsummer Night's Dream*, Bizet for Daudet's *L'Arlésienne* and Grieg for *Peer Gynt*. Nobody peered around and asked, "Where is the orchestra coming from?" when they listened to such scores as these.

The only exception that was made in the early days of sound pictures in Hollywood was in musical comedies, where the girl walked into the room where the boy was seated at the piano. He would say, "Listen to this tune I just wrote . . ." whereupon she would sing it from the second bar on with every word in the lyric perfect. How many times I have envied the telepathic abilities of Jeanette MacDonald, Grace Moore, Lily Pons, Gladys Swarthout and the rest—especially after I found out how long it takes them actually to learn a tune.

However, my first experiences in Hollywood had nothing to do with music. I was hired (in 1929) as an actor, to play the part of a pianist in the screen version of *Burlesque*. I had played the role in the Arthur Hopkins production on Broadway, and it was the intention of the producing company to retain most of the original cast, only replacing Barbara Stanwyck with Nancy Carroll. I had utterly no desire to go to Hollywood, as I had just signed a song-writing contract with Max Dreyfuss at Harms. So the producer offered me "twice as much." This was mysterious to me, as my reluctance had nothing to do with the money I had been offered. My acceptance after this "twice-as-much" temptation had everything to do with it, however. The picture was made (for Paramount) as *The Dance of Life*—with no apologies to the late Havelock Ellis, though his fee for the title went into five figures.

Through the association with Dreyfuss my activities thereafter shifted to R.K.O. The vice-president in charge of production was William Le Baron, another émigré from Broadway, where he had written the lyrics for *Apple Blossoms*, among other chores. Through the friendly word spoken for me by Dreyfuss I was assigned to write several songs for *Street Girl*, the first talkie produced by R.K.O. Among them was "Lovable and Sweet," which was a big hit. However, in those days practically anything that got into a picture was a big hit.

I began to broaden out in my talents after this, becoming in fact a right-hand man for Le Baron, especially during the period prior to the production of *Cimarron*. I sat in on many conferences in which an actress for the leading feminine role was being discussed. I didn't know whom they should choose, but I was emphatically opposed to Irene Dunne, arguing that she was not the type. When this turned out to be the biggest money-maker in the firm's history and a personal triumph for Dunne, somehow I found myself doing more and more music again.

In as much as *Street Girl* was an early venture by R.K.O. they had no actual "music department" for the film. The producer just hired Gus Arnheim's band to play the score because it happened that he was playing at the Coconut Grove in Los Angeles at the time. All that was done was to map out a routine for the band on the tunes—first chorus saxes, second vocal, third brass and so on—and let them play it. Then the same sound track was repeated over and over, as many as half-a-dozen times in the picture. It was used for the main title, the end title and even for the trailer. They certainly got their money's worth out of that one chorus. The elaborate scoring that is now a commonplace even in cartoon pictures was then unheard of in Hollywood.

It was during this period, at the crest of the boom years, that New York musical talent began to migrate to the coast, lured by that "twice-as-much" psychology. First all the available popular-song writers were hired to write "tunes." Then as a step higher in the aesthetic scale the producers turned to show composers. Characteristically, they got the unimportant ones first. It was not until almost the end of the first music cycle that Kern, Rodgers and Romberg were brought out; and, as everybody knows, Fox actually had Gershwin on their hands writing "Delicious" when that cycle stopped revolving.

Through Le Baron and Dreyfuss R.K.O. became virtually a West Coast agency for Dillingham talent. One of the first fairly well known show composers to work for the films was Harry Tierney, composer of *Irene*, *Kid Boots* and numerous other scores, who was imported to embellish his *Rio Rita*, then about to be filmed, with a few new tunes. Either by temporary or permanent standards, this was an event of practically no importance at all—save that Tierney insisted on bringing along with him his own orchestrator, by name, Max Steiner.

This was the beginning, in a word, of a dynasty. You recall perhaps the poignant background music for *The Informer?* That was Steiner. The distant dissonant trumpets in *The Lost Patrol?* Also Steiner. The undercurrent of music in *Four Daughters?* The tortured death music of *Angels with Dirty Faces?* These, and the sounds, effects and suggestive noises of a hundred other films were all by Max Steiner.

A little man who is incessantly making questionable puns, Steiner, pre-Hollywood, was the kind of a conductor that a producer of musical comedies always thought of third. He would be called in to conduct if the two conductors you had thought of first couldn't be had. An overrich orchestrator for the theater, Steiner's abilities in this field were suitable for occasional spots but not for a whole musical comedy. Since no continuous scoring was being used in Hollywood during the early days of the talkies—the formula being to devise a few motives that appeared at the beginning, in the middle and at the end of the picture (surely you haven't forgotten the vogue for "theme songs" in even such dramatic films as *Seventh Heaven, Diane, What Price Glory* or *Charmaine*) Steiner found himself in a milieu almost tailored to his talents.

However, Steiner's position was not established in any such simple way as this coincidence of talents and a situation suggests. He found an early opportunity for "creative" writing in preparing R.K.O. pictures for the Spanish market (both transatlantic and South American) attaining quite a reputation in the trade for this. Spanish actors were employed to speak Spanish dialogue vaguely paralleling the original texts of the pictures, but as they never utilized nearly so many words as the original script specified there remained many *lacunae* which Steiner filled with music scored for a six-piece orchestra.

This was about 1929. That Steiner has remained in Hollywood during the years since then and prospered suggests that his talents were early recognized and established as indispensable. The truth is rather more prosaic. It chanced that shortly after this the first "music cycle" in Hollywood history came to an end, and virtually all the high-priced musicians were released at the end of their contracts, thereafter returning to New York. Steiner did not qualify for inclusion in this category, and his services were retained. Thus he had the opportunity to develop with the talkies as the attitude toward music gradually grew more tolerant.

This was slow progress and not without its digressions. The level of musical perception among Hollywood producers is, if anything, slightly lower than their perception of values associated with the other arts. Curiously, the humble artisans who are great music lovers (meaning that they will stand for six hours to hear Gigli in *Pagliacci*) never seem to be the humble artisans who become movie producers.

I recall the plight of one, whose social prestige decreed his presence at a certain Hollywood Bowl concert. It chanced that the important work of the evening was the C minor symphony of Beethoven, which he suffered in silence until the coda of the final movement. This has, as you will recall, what could be described as an 1805 Roxy finish, with the tonic and dominant chords repeated a dozen times, with flourishes. At each insistent recurrence of the tonic he half rose from his chair to facilitate his exit . . . also because he was bored. When the third series of tonic and dominant chords still left him short of the actual end of the movement he turned and muttered, "The rat fooled me again."

On this same program was a two-piano concerto by Mozart, which he dismissed with the terse comment, "It never got anywhere."

Sometime later, after a performance of Ravel's "Bolero" at the Bowl, I received a memo telling me to report the following morning at nine, because "he had an idea." This, apparently, was the one thing he heard during the whole summer that stimulated him. To enhance his position in Hollywood cultural life, he offered a musicale one night at which the invited performers were the Compinsky Trio. They were in excellent form, playing trios by Brahms, Arensky and Franck to the considerable pleasure of the guests.

However, just as the applause of the listeners seemed about to result in an encore the host stepped forward —as if anticipating their intention—and said briskly,

"All right, boys—that's enough."

Perhaps his most searching bit of musical criticism was propounded when he said to me dictatorially, "In my opinion"—marking the words carefully to allow the full weight of his thought to rest on me—"the greatest piece of music ever written is 'Humoreske.'"

It was after such a characteristic demonstration that S. N. Behrman said of this producer, "Now I know why he can make those instantaneous decisions—he is never deflected by thought."

That Steiner was able to make any substantial headway against such resistance is a tribute almost as much to his patience as to his talents. From the making of shorts (one of which won him, in some obscure way, the small red ribbon with all the incidental prerogatives of the *Légion d'Honneur*) he progressed to more substantial accomplishments. Possibly the first general notice that was accorded his work came when the Academy Award was bestowed on *The Informer*, with an incidental citation for Steiner's score, though his capacities were recognized in the trade before this, particularly for his work on *The Lost Patrol*.

It was during this period of emergence that Steiner began to come into conflict with his producers as his passion for illuminating action with sound developed, and his position at the studio strengthened. He would seize upon every new script that came into the office, searching it through to find strange new uses for music. Anything with lightning and thunder or a few good horror episodes automatically became Steiner's property. I doubt, however, that even he dreamed of so ideal a fulfillment of his hopes as he encountered in *King Kong*. This *really* got him.

It offered him a chance to write the kind of music no one had ever heard before—or since. Full of weird chords, strident background noises, rumblings and heavings, it was one of the most enthusiastically written scores ever to be composed in Hollywood. Indeed, it was always my feeling that it should have been advertised as a concert of Steiner's music with accompanying pictures on the screen. To return to Katherine Hepburn after scoring for mountains, monsters, armies and jungles must have seemed rather piddling.

A peculiarity of Steiner's scores is that his orchestrator must always provide a part for the harp—and a good one. This caused some difficulty in the life of Robert Russell Bennett, when he came West to orchestrate Jerome Kern's *I Dream Too Much*, in which Lily Pons was starred. This was altogether a confusing picture, because it was conducted by Steiner, who was also a composer, orchestrated by Bennett (whom Steiner never particularly liked to have around, as it reminded him too keenly of the days at Harms when he was the number-three orchestrator behind Bennett) and starred Pons, who insisted on having André Kostelanetz conduct her sequences.

Possibly to escape some of this concantenation of temperaments, Bennett did his orchestrating in Montana, sending in each number as it was completed. Not aware of Steiner's penchant for the harp, he omitted that instrument from the scoring of the title song, a chromatic waltz and thus not suited to the harp. Immediately there came a telegram from Steiner:

"Why no harp part?"

After puzzling over this for an hour Bennett reached a conclusion and wired back, "If there's a charming girl you want to use, put in a harp part."

The inevitable P.S. is that there was a "charming girl," who is now Steiner's wife.

It chanced that I was also working at the R.K.O. studios at the time, doing a score for Ginger Rogers' *In Person*, and I helped out on some of the technical details for *I Dream Too Much*. Essentially this was an outgrowth of my old hero-worship for Kern, a feeling shared by virtually all song writers. When Pons came to make her sound tracks she made several recordings of each difficult high note which was first played for her on the piano. Then they used the best note, splicing the sound tracks back and forth to achieve the perfect result you heard in the theater. It's a technique that the Metropolitan might look into.

My presence at R.K.O. was in part a consequence of the meteoric rise of Pan Berman, who, during my early Le Baron days, was a head cutter at the studio and very fresh—not in the sense that a flower is. At the time of which I'm speaking he was producing films there. Just at the end of the singer cycle Berman was contemplating the use of Pons in another film, rather more ambitious musically, but was not quite sure in his own mind whether to do so or not. In an effort to determine just how great her qualities were he would play records for me by the hour of Galli-Curci, Tetrazzini and Pons, quizzing me after each, "Who was that?"

To me, knowing nothing of any coloratura, they were all equally brilliant and equally flat. Eventually (after I had heard the "Bell Song" some eighteen or

twenty times) I began to feel like a Cuban general en-
dorsing a five-cent cigar.

My job on *In Person* consisted mainly of writing
several songs, for which I was hired on a guarantee
spread over weekly periods of payment. During an
amiable lunch with Berman one day at the studio
(when my work was ended, though I was still doing
some advisory bits on the picture) he said, "The thing
is running way over the budget. It's costing us an
awful lot, and it 'll be worse if I don't find some way of
cutting down." He looked at me amiably and said,
"You're fired."

The abruptness of this startled me, but I was even
more puzzled when I thought it over subsequently,
because I was getting less than anybody else on the
staff.

I left Hollywood for New York before the cutting
was completed and didn't get to see *In Person* until a
preview just before the opening. Later that evening I
met Berman for dinner, and he started by asking me
how I liked the picture.

"Frankly, Pan," I said, "I was disappointed."

He rose from the table in a rage, flung down his
napkin and said, "Who in hell are *you* to be disappointed?"

The discussion of who had to be who to be disappointed took quite a long time.

Despite the vagaries of Steiner he must be credited with the establishment of certain basic principles in movie scoring, particularly through his knack of "catching things" musically. Such is the music, in his score for *Of Human Bondage*, that paralleled Philip's limp. It was almost a crippled theme, so exactly did it correspond to the hesitation in the character's walk. The secret of this derives from Steiner's painstaking study of the scenes for which he is to write music, his mathematical analysis of them in terms of "clicks."

This is a technique now used universally in writing movie music, though six years or so ago it was a novelty. By breaking down the footage of a picture into separate scenes the composer can then calculate exactly the number of seconds for so many feet of film and then write precisely that much music to cover the episode he wants to illuminate. Naturally there is the problem of dubbing the music onto the sound track so that it corresponds to incidents in the picture, but that can be done faultlessly by synchronizing the conductor's beat with the speed of the film.

In a sense this might be described as the "Mickey-Mouse" technique, in which every movement of the character on the screen has a complementary bar of music. Steiner is particularly adept at this sort of thing, though his heavy-handed impressionism does not serve him too well in more subjective situations. He is, however, an excellent man on prison-break fogs, and also does a good job of industrial noises. Do you recall the whistles, bells, clanging of doors and other institutional sounds for *Crime School?* The hammer blows and engine noises in *Dodge City?* They were all a part of Steiner's score for these films, and enormously effective.

Up to the time he wrote the music for *Alice Adams* (which was the last close contact I had with him) Steiner's consuming passion was—for a man who had written the vast quantities of music he had—a paradoxical one. He wanted to have something published. Essentially a utilitarian composer, Steiner's work went directly from his worktable (by way of a mimeographing process) to the music stands of the orchestra, without even the dubious permanence that comes from the engraving of a plate and the solid feeling of a sheet of music in the hand. With all his composing I doubt that he ever had the ten published songs necessary to get him into A.S.C.A.P. (The American Society of Composers, Authors and Publishers). Naturally it was a great source of irritation to him, one of the busiest composers in the country, to be excluded from this society. However, symphony orchestras rarely play movie music, and the market for "agitatos" could hardly be described as ready.

Steiner's subsequent ambition is unknown to me save as it was confided in the course of the discussion, recently, of a new work he was writing—a symphony. Expostulating, and with vehemence, he declared, "It'll be either the God-damnedest hit or the biggest flop *you* ever heard." Since I had heard many performances of new symphonies, none of which fitted comfortably into either of these categories, I could only conclude that he was giving birth to something unusual indeed.

Steiner's "Mickey-Mouse" technique is firmly entrenched in Hollywood, but it also has a robust opponent in another method prevailing in Hollywood, in which the composer doesn't bother to "catch" anything. This might be called the "over-all" or "mood" treatment, in which the endeavor is merely to suggest the whole atmosphere of a sequence with just a few main motives.

Thus, in a triangle picture, you have a "spiritual love" theme, the "other woman" theme, and probably a motive for "conflict." Alfred Newman is a disciple of this school, which derives from Tschaikowsky by way of whole tones. It has always impressed me, however, that the "other woman" theme is generally more exciting, a good deal more enthusiastically written, than the one for the wife. There are constant arguments between the partisans for each method of procedure, the only agreement being that it is more difficult to write in the "Mickey-Mouse" manner than in the "over-all" style. On the other hand, it can be contended that a good lush motive for a dramatic situation requires more real creative talent than the other kind of writing.

However, as the increasing prominence of music in pictures has greatly extended the number of employed composers in Hollywood, there is plentiful opportunity for writers of both types. There are now few pictures of any kind that do not utilize music to some degree, and in a considerable majority of them the score is credited to a musician of specialized, if not general reputation. Offhand, in the last year, I have seen films from Hollywood with scores attributed to Richard Hageman, Louis Gruenberg, Ernst Toch, Kurt Weill, W. Franke Harling, George Antheil, Erich Korngold and Werner Janssen, all composers of general reputation; as well as others by such specialists as Steiner, Newman, Stothart, Franz Waxman, Edward Ward, Hugo Friedhofer and Edward Powell, to mention only the more familiar names. Indeed, the methods of mass production have in few other connections been utilized with the skill with which they are applied to the writing of movie scores in Hollywood.

I had an unenviable opportunity to come closely into contact with those methods several years ago during one of my more recent Hollywood intervals. I had tired of living on the periphery of asceticism while studying with Schoenberg and sought employment with a movie company, convinced that I could copy as capably from Debussy and Delius as anyone then active in the films.

Through the intercession of friends I was provided with an introduction to an official at M.G.M., whom I had also met on previous occasions at various parties. At one of these, impressed by some fugitive manifestation of talent, he said, "Come to see me. I want to do something for you."

It was after this that I came with the introduction. He looked at me with evident disinterest while he listened to a recitation of my background. Then he shook my hand encouragingly and said,

"Yes. Come back again in two months."

Just what I was supposed to do in this interim was not made clear. But while I awaited the expiration of this interlocutory degree of divorce from my unemployment my friends continued the program of propaganda on my behalf. Finally I was granted a second interview and again rehearsed my qualifications. My prospective employer (so I visualized him) listened with impolite inattentiveness, continuously saying, "Yes? Yes?"

Finally he turned and said, "I'll have to refer you to our music director, Nat Finston."

I had had some dealings with Finston at the Rivoli Theater in New York years before when he was a conductor there. I found him in a commodious office, hung with charts which were his most absorbing possession. Within a few minutes he had led me to the wall (which they covered completely) and begun to explain their significance. Each chart represented a film, and each bore the name of a composer who had been assigned to write the score for it. There was one for Stothart, another for Ward, a third for Waxman and so on. As Commissar of Music for the M.G.M. enterprises, Finston was as closely in touch with the activities of his vassals as the tovarisch in charge of a salt mine in the Ukraine.

He then launched into a long exposition of his career at the studio, detailing the chaos in which he found the music department and the perfection of organization that now prevailed.

"I tell you," he said, "it's running like a well-oiled machine."

The phrase appealed to him, and he repeated,

"Like a well-oiled machine. Every man a cog in the wheel."

Then he looked at me severely—running his hands through his thick hair as he did and pacing the room with supervisory strides—and said, "I don't know whether or not you would fit in."

"Mr Finston," I answered, "my greatest desire in life at this moment is to be a cog in the wheel. If I don't qualify it will be because my music is inferior, not because I don't want to be a cog in the wheel."

In response he suggested that I bring in a few scores for him to see.

I came back the next day with my scores, and before I was aware of what was happening we were again busy with the well-oiled machine and how important it was to be a cog in the wheel. The exposition was even more detailed than that of the previous day, though no new territory was explored. The purely scientific pleasure that Finston derived from his creation obviously excluded any interruptions from me. At the end of his discourse he shook his head, implying doubt, and said, "I don't think you'd fit into this well-oiled machine." Then he added as a kind of consolation award, "But any time you want call me up, and we'll have a chat."

It was not until I was outside that I realized that my scores were in the same package in which I had brought them, that Finston had never looked at them.

Two days later I rang up M.G.M. and asked to be connected with Mr Finston. At length I got through to him, and he said brusquely,

"I'm busy. What's on your mind?"

"Nothing," I said. "I just would like to have a chat."

Annoyed but still not quite knowing whether he should show it or not, Finston exclaimed, "Some other time. Not now."

This, in an anecdote, was the history of my career as a composer with M.G.M.

At an opposite, but not much more inviting pole, was my experience with Ben Hecht and Charles MacArthur when they were producing pictures in the East. Specifically, it was during the making of *Crime without Passion*, for which I wrote some of the music—

only the brittle, disillusioned parts, not the big tuttis. These were done by Frank Tours, music director of the picture. My association with Hecht arose from the fact that I was at liberty, and he played the violin very badly. As hardly more than a gag, he offered me $15 to play duets with him once a week. I accepted and found myself becoming engrossed in his producing activities.

Since Tours was so busy he gave me several sequences to write, and I became very much immersed in the film, going to the studio daily. Since I was living at a mid-town hotel, and the studio was in Astoria, my cab fares found me losing about eight dollars a week on the fifteen. Hecht, satirizing Hollywood studios, gave everyone important titles. The office boys were all members of the board of directors, the porter was Supervisor in Charge of Sanitation, and I, the only other person in the music department beside Tours, was installed as Assistant President of the Music Department.

Despite the burden of this honor I found it necessary to go to Hecht one day and point out that I was losing money on the job. With a generous gesture he nominally doubled my salary each week, though my pay check still called for only $15. It seemed that the checks had to go through five banks and the hands of ten suspicious people who were backing him.

Nevertheless this did not alleviate my situation, and to placate me, Hecht kept sending a steady stream of memos announcing increases in my wage. One day I was drawing $350 a week. An hour later I received a memo announcing that I had been raised to $500. By the end of the week my salary had mounted to $1200, but there still was only $15 in my pay envelope. There then ensued a series of weekly raises, to a rhythm of $500 a week. Before long I was in the hysterical brackets, but still only drawing my $15.

Finally I went to his office one day and said,

"I can't afford any more of these raises. I'm starving to death as it is."

Whether one would consider this an experience as a cog in a machine, well-oiled or otherwise, is at least debatable. However, I had such an opportunity a little later when, through the intercession of Irving Berlin, I was tapped for membership at Twentieth Century-Fox. But again I was frustrated. Since I had been hired as a composer through an executive channel I had little contact with the actual music department, which was supervised by Lou Silvers. He avoided giving me any assignment to work under him, being—as he remarked to one of his associates—afraid of my jokes. All during the time I was employed there Silvers lived in fear that I might make him the object of a wisecrack.

The presiding genius of Twentieth Century-Fox is, of course, Daryll Zanuck, who might be described as a man who knows, unfortunately, what he wants. From the tradition of ignorance of all music that had prevailed during the early years of sound films, there had grown up another belief, which held that a producer should know a little about everything that went into a picture—history, grammar, costume, design, dramaturgy, even music. This opens an endless vista of prediction. In such a picture as *Under Two Flags*—which was not a mere epic but a super-spectacle—Zanuck decreed that the musical score should include, as its basic elementals, Cui's "Orientale" and the "Chanson Arabe" from Tschaikowsky's "Nutcracker" suite. This he referred to as "something they could whistle." (I never did find out who was meant by "they.")

It was this type of erudition that was displayed by another producer (not Zanuck) who was in charge of a picture with a Parisian background. He came to an audition of one extended bit of music that was designed to accompany the main character on a stroll along a boulevard in Paris (the high point of the film, musically). He gave his best critical attention to the playing of the orchestra, and when it was finished, pausing reflectively, he said, "Not bad. Not bad. But it's not Frenchy enough."

Suddenly he roused himself from his deep thought, snapped his fingers and said,

"I've got it! Put in a few more French horns."

As a digression I might mention that Zanuck was a man with a somewhat sadistic sense of humor. His particular penchant was for satirical practical jokes. While *Lloyds of London* was in the discussion state he conceived a *jeu d'esprit* that took account of the fancy which inhabited the soul of the late Sam Pokrass, composer, that he was a gifted gag man. This delusion was somewhat complicated by the difficulty that impeded the Russian-born Pokrass' use of the English language. He reminded me of the prize-fight manager of whom Dan Parker, savant of the *Daily Mirror* said, "His mother tongue is broken English."

He called in Pokrass and outlined the story to him, explaining that it was a project for the Ritz Brothers, and indicating that it needed a bit of sprucing up with gags and comedy situations. Poor Pokrass spent two weeks trying to brighten up the script of *Lloyds of London* with gags for the Ritz Brothers before word seeped through to him that the stars of it were Tyrone Power, Virginia Field and Robert Sanders!

With Twentieth Century-Fox, one of my early undertakings was to write an operatic sequence for *Charlie Chan at the Opera* (not, however, *Le Crayon sur le table*). This was due to my friendship with John Stone, who was in charge of the production. Since this was a B film there were certain problems to be met, especially those of the budget. Twentieth Century-Fox had just completed an elaborate spectacle with Lawrence Tibbett, of which one of the high spots was a *Faust* scene in which the star wore a magnificent Mephistophelian costume.

One of our first problems arose when the costume was assigned to *Charlie Chan at the Opera*, with instructions for us to put it to work. I had heard of music being written around a singer, but never for a costume. Nevertheless, determined to become a cog in the wheel, I set myself to writing an operatic sequence in which the big aria found a baritone wearing this elegant Mephistopheles costume. As an additional slight detail it was necessary for the aria to work up to a point at which the singer stabbed the girl with a lethal knife malevolently substituted for the prop one. This was the whole point of the picture.

[117]

Since we had no libretto I wrote the music first, and then the words were written for it by Bill Kernell, a lyricist who also wrote songs. He was assigned to the job because it was thought that he would have more musical understanding than the ordinary hack writer. I never did find out the meaning of the silly English words he wrote for the music, because as soon as he was finished studio linguists were called in to translate the whole thing into Italian.

In addition to this baritone aria (which came out as a potent mingling of Moussorgsky and pure Levant) I also wrote a soprano scene, rather lyrical and expressive, also a rhythmic little march for some soldiers that we introduced into the episode. (The lead role, that of the baritone, was played by Boris Karloff, though the voice was dubbed, of course.) My only specification in writing the score was that at some point I should be able to use the word "silencio," which always appealed to me. They compromised by letting me begin one aria with "Silencio!"

Having had little experience in writing opera, I asked Schoenberg for some advice. He advised me to study the score of Beethoven's *Fidelio*. Since this is one of the most unoperatic of all operas it was just what I didn't need.

In the idiom I used there were a few turns of phrase which I considered individual, also a harmonic idiom a little more adventurous than that commonly encountered in such writing. It was acceptable to the producers (they liked the soprano aria particularly because it had a good tune) but I encountered some difficulty with the orchestral players. I was especially irritated with one of the violinists, who took exception to the way I had written a certain phrase, saying, "My finger doesn't want to go there."

Among the musicians with whom I came in contact was Herbert Spencer, a remarkable orchestrator, who is greatly admired by his co-workers, including me. He was known especially as a "sound" man. All the orchestrators came to him when they had difficulties, to make sure that a certain texture of orchestration would "sound" when it was played.

Spencer was, by some curiosity, a Chilean—and even more remarkably—a blond Chilean. He was sent by his parents to study engineering at the University of Pennsylvania but digressed into playing the saxophone. From this he went on to play with Vincent Lopez and to arrange for him. He studied for a time with Floridia, who was among other distinctions the teacher of Nat Shilkret—of whom I'll dispose with just the mention of his name. After this, Spencer spent a few mathematical afternoons with Joseph Schillinger. Then he passed into radio work, doing the Burns and Allen show for Bobby Dolan. When the comedians went to Hollywood to work, Spencer came along to do their orchestrating. At length, by these devious paths, he went into pictures, acquiring a considerable reputation as a specialist. One of his best jobs was the orchestration of Irving Berlin's "On the Avenue."

The other well-respected orchestrators in Hollywood were hardly less eclectic in background. Edward Powell was brought out by Alfred Newman, who plucked him from the Harms-Chappell training school, where he had done among other jobs the orchestration of Gershwin's *Let 'Em Eat Cake.* Carroll Huxley, one of the best arrangers for Kostelanetz and Whiteman, was drawn from radio. For some obscure reason he was assigned to score for Westerns, which did no good either for Huxley or for the Westerns. His career in pictures was not very lengthy. Robert Russell Bennett, of course, had perhaps the most conspicuous reputation as an orchestrator for the Broadway theater of any man in America, having done splendid work in such shows as *Show Boat* and *The Band Wagon.* He never particularly relished working in

[120]

Hollywood, going there principally out of friendship for Kern, with whom he has worked for many years.

I speak of these boys particularly because they share a common background of training on Broadway and almost all of them were Harms alumni. There were other fine orchestrators in Hollywood, one among them being Ray Heindorf at Warner Brothers. He was noted especially for his work on musical pictures, being a wonderful hand at orchestrating song choruses, dance routines and similar work.

Much of the fine work these men do is conditioned by the characteristics of sound-track recording. I don't know whether their work would come off nearly so well without a microphone. (This does not apply at all to Bennett, who is much more flexible.) A clarinet against six brass is all right if the clarinet can walk up to the microphone and play his solo there. It is another problem to score for the concert hall, where such an effect would be lost completely.

While at Twentieth Century-Fox I also came into contact with the remarkable custom (considering the species of human that inhabited the music department) of tea with the usual "trumpets" each afternoon at five. Everybody in the music department had to contribute a certain sum each week for the Tea Fund.

There was also a communal approach to other problems, notably the one of keeping abreast of developments elsewhere in the musical world. The boys obtained every important new score as soon as it was available, with the result that Hindemith's "Mathis der Maler" was known in Hollywood before it was played in Carnegie Hall. They frequently had meetings at each other's houses, where they would play records, break down the instrumentation of certain passages, discuss the technique of the writing and make notes on the effects that were introduced in the scores.

The effect of this was not invisible in their own scores. It was with more than a slight feeling of surprise that I listened to the pattern of Ravel's "La Valse" as the background to a brilliant treatment of a Cole Porter song in *Rosalie*. For Spanish things the treatment is generally influenced by Debussy's "Iberia" or the Arbos orchestration of Albeniz's "Triana." After a time the boys got hold of a few Villa-Lobos records. They did all right with those, too. The Spanish port of call in Ibert's "Escales" has not been overlooked, either.

Two types of orchestration have come into such general use in Hollywood that I began the custom of referring to them as "generic" or "derivative." "Generic" is something that sounds like something else.

"Derivative," however, is a term of stronger censure implying that you have lifted the whole texture from some not-too-familiar source.

I should mention that Delius was discovered in Hollywood about three years ago. It immediately became the standard thing for walks in the garden, bicycle rides or the English downs at dawn. Another orchestrator, David Raksin, was affected in a far-reaching way by the scherzo of the Shostakovitch first symphony.

Raksin was one of my favorite Hollywood musicians. We went frequently to the Bowl together, where he would tell me that the tuba bothered him, accoustically—even though we sat a full mile from the stage. His secret ambition was to be a ballet dancer, and he also wrote papers on accoustics for scientific magazines. He, too, was originally a saxophonist, thereafter playing and arranging for Al Goodman before passing into the Chappell net.

Raksin came to Hollywood primarily to take down Chaplin's whistling of his own score for *Modern Times*. Since the whistling method of composing is a rather tenuous thing, and in any case Chaplin's whistling is at best pretty derivative, the difficulties of such a collaboration may be imagined. It was arduous

[123]

enough for Raksin to sit all day waiting for Chaplin to whistle, without the further complications of that artist's temperament. The inevitable thing happened, but Newman patched up the argument, and Raksin went back to taking down Chaplin's whistling. I never could understand how one might whistle harmony and counterpoint as well as a tune. Under any circumstances it seems a complicated approach to composition. However, together with his great gifts in other directions, Chaplin combines a facility in this direction.

Newman—who is the best conductor by far in Hollywood—had a tremendous argument with Chaplin over the directing of the score of *Modern Times*. Being independent as well as able, Newman walked out on the job, and Eddie Powell was called in to direct the last reel. Apparently Newman found that the whistling type of composer is more trying by far than Stravinsky and Schoenberg together.

At Twentieth Century-Fox, Louis Silvers was in charge of the musical affairs. He did no composing himself, confining himself to conducting and supervising. Somewhat disturbed by the newer trends in movie music, he fortified himself by securing the services of the fine Austrian modernist, Ernst Toch. Silvers never actually utilized his talents to write a film but kept him as a kind of Toch in the hole, in case Steiner or Newman put over something revolutionary in one of their pictures.

Toch had had some experience as a composer for the films both in England and America. Abroad, he had composed the score for *Little Friend* (with Nova Pillbeam) but the experience did not please him too much. It was his contention that the producers had used only the lower part of his orchestration, omitting everything in the upper staves. In Hollywood, his experience was principally concerned with a film version of *Peter Ibbetson* at Paramount. However, his score was considerably "touched up" by Hugo Friedhofer in order to make it serviceable for the film within the allotted time and to conform to the technical means at hand. Friedhofer subsequently embarked on a course of study with Toch and became one of his best pupils.

There is rarely a period in Hollywood when all the orchestrators and most of the movie composers are not studying with one or another of the prominent musicians who have gone there to live recently. At one time the vogue was for Schoenberg, who came with a great reputation, of course, as a teacher. However, most of the boys wanted to take a six weeks' course and learn a handful of Schoenberg tricks. They were sorely disappointed when they discovered that it was his intention to give them instruction in counterpoint, harmony and chorale, which meant that they would have to expend considerable effort themselves in doing assigned work.

One especially naïve young man took one of his problems to Schoenberg, hopeful of a quick, concise solution. He had been assigned to write some music for an airplane sequence and was not sure how he should go about it. He posed the problem to Schoenberg, who thought for a moment and then said,

"Airplane music? Just like music for big bees, only louder."

He afterwards always referred to this kind of music as "big bee" music.

When Schoenberg arrived in California it was the desire of his friends to see him employed in the movies and well paid for it. He was invited to an important première, following which the producer intercepted him and asked what he thought of the score. Schoenberg replied that he hadn't noticed it, thus bearing out the average producer's theory of what constitutes a good score, only in reverse.

Nevertheless, his friends continued the propaganda, one of the most active among them being Salka Viertel. She knew that Thalberg had *Good Earth* in preparation and subtly implanted the idea in his mind of utilizing Schoenberg to write the score. He was singularly unimpressed with her tales of his eminence until she chanced to mention that there was a considerable article about Schoenberg in the Encyclopaedia Brittanica. When he had confirmed the information his interest in Schoenberg immediately became acute.

It chanced then that the Columbia Broadcasting System was presenting a broadcast in Schoenberg's honor, of which a principal work was his early "Verklärte Nacht." Its romantic flavor and poetic character deeply impressed Thalberg, who thereafter sent an emissary to see Schoenberg, even though the music he might write now would have no possible resemblance to "Verklärte Nacht." The emissary found the composer indifferent to the idea and thereupon launched into a long recitation of the possibilities for music in the film, leading up to a dramatic exposition of its "big scene."

"Think of it!" he enthused. "There's a terrific storm going on, the wheat field is swaying in the wind, and suddenly the earth begins to tremble. In the midst of the earthquake Oo-Lan gives birth to a baby. What an opportunity for music!"

"With so much going on," said Schoenberg mildly, "what do you need music for?"

Some time after my Twentieth Century-Fox experiences I established a contact with David Selznick, who also knew—more or less—what he wanted. This also permitted a sentimental reunion with Ben Hecht, for my assignment was to his amusing *Nothing Sacred,* with Fredric March and Carole Lombard.

If I appeared at the studio with anything even faintly modern Selznick's invariable comment was,

"It sounds Chinese."

On the other hand, if I produced something that was not obviously melodic, but well written for the orchestra, his reaction was,

"You're not writing for the Bowl. You're writing for fifty million people."

To him, the Bowl represented the pinnacle of everything that was erudite in music—a combination of the Paris Conservatoire, Carnegie Hall and the Mozarteum in Salzburg, occupying an empty space on a hillside. It was a place you went to if you wanted to assure yourself of a dull evening. Despite this he has a very creative part in supervising the music used in his pictures.

Personally, however, I always enjoyed amiable relations with Selznick. He had a weakness for me, perhaps because I came from Pittsburgh, where he originated, and also because his brother Myron had a fondness for me. Through me Selznick was enabled to become a fractional patron of the arts. He became interested in my activities as a composer, and even after my work at the studio was completed I continued to have a modest drawing account so that I could continue with my serious work. In return I eventually gave him some musical material for *Made for Each Other*, in which Carole Lombard and James Stewart appeared.

Before this, however, I had left Hollywood to come East, without knowing just what Selznick would want of me. He wrote to say that I should just collect some themes so that they would be available when he needed them. I responded in a letter that this was rather a confusing assignment, leaving a good deal of latitude for both of us. In return Selznick wrote that if my music came up to the level of my letter he would be thoroughly satisfied.

There are few men in Hollywood so completely devoted to their pictures as Selznick. He represents the second generation of a Hollywood Royal Family and takes tremendous pride in his work. Nothing he produces costs less than two million dollars, for he feels that it would not otherwise be worthy of the Selznick traditions. It is rumored, indeed, that he left M.G.M. to establish his own firm so that the name of Selznick would be perpetuated in pictures.

I have referred at various points in this chapter to composers and orchestrators as separate individuals, which might be slightly confusing to the uninitiated. This is only appropriate, however, as there are few things more confusing than the means by which a score is created in Hollywood, even to the initiated. Few composers, for example, do their own orchestration. The scattered exceptions are the orchestrators who become composers. The distinction is that a composer like Steiner or Newman or Stothart will lay out the orchestration and sketch the effects that he has in mind. Thereafter his orchestrator will do the work of actually working out the instrumentation, of filling in the background texture. In some instances a composer will just give the themes to the orchestrator and let him play around with them according to a predesignated outline.

The business of orchestrating has become so specialized that a good orchestrator, if he is rushed with several jobs, will give out the orchestration to other orchestrators, unbeknown to the composer. The orchestrators are paid by the page, about $5.00 (no page contains more than four bars, by union specifications). This is the minimum rate, and if a well-known orchestrator is paid a premium for his services he can farm out some of his work to a less expensive man and still make a profit on the deal. De luxe orchestrators, such as Robert Russell Bennett, are hired for a specific job against a guarantee. If the amount of orchestration exceeds a specified number of pages they are paid *pro rata* for the excess pages.

The composers, on the other hand, are paid (for the run-of-the-mine jobs) by the minute in most studios. The number of minutes of music used—generally specified in advance—determines the payment the composer receives for his job. A reasonable figure for this type of work would be about $200 a minute. It is apparent that this is excellent pay for slow, sustained music. (I never could get away with much of that slow-chord stuff.) However, if you are required to write a few scherzos, or battle music that goes very fast or a score for a chase, it doesn't work out so well.

Sometimes after a distinguished career an orchestrator will be promoted to the status of a composer. Eddie Powell and Hugo Friedhofer, for example, wrote a film together for Hal Roach. In such circumstances, naturally, the orchestrators will do their own orchestration. As I have pointed out, Max Steiner began his career in Hollywood as an orchestrator, rising later to his more exalted status.

Much of this division of labor arises from the circumstances that govern the production of the average picture. The element of time is perhaps the most important of all. For, it must be understood, no score for a Hollywood picture is written until the movie is virtually completed. It is not until the film is cut and assembled that the composer knows where the best opportunities will be for his music and how to plan the effects that will best enhance the film. Since a comparatively short time elapses between the completion of the average film and its release the composer has to work expeditiously. Thus the composer hardly has time for his own orchestrating, even if he knows how; and furthermore, no important composer—Steiner, Newman, Stothart—would consider it worth his while to bother orchestrating when some specialist can do it as well or better for a stipulated sum.

Of course, once the composer has been assigned to a picture he might look in on it during production or even read the script, thereafter collecting themes or motives to be whipped into shape when the time for his writing arrives. Some composers prefer to work this way, while others do very little until they see the film in the projection room, going on from there.

In the first class, I think particularly of Erich Wolfgang—for Mozart—Korngold. This was exemplified during the production of *Midsummer Night's Dream*, for which he had been hired to reorchestrate Mendelssohn's score and add some new material. As he entered the studio yard one day on the way to his office a car drove up and James Cagney, who played Bottom in the film, stepped out. It chanced that Cagney and Korngold had not met previously, and the flunkey who was guiding Korngold about thought this would be a favorable opportunity to bring the two together.

Korngold had no sooner been presented to Cagney than he stepped back and said, "Hold still, Mr Cagney. Hold still a minute."

Then he rubbed his chin reflectively and began to hum a little. Walking around to the other side, he continued the inspection and the humming, meanwhile whistling contentedly under his breath. Finally, when the image of Cagney had been securely captured in musical terms, he thanked his subject and departed.

Cagney said he almost felt as if he should ask when

to come in and try on the theme for which Korngold had fitted him.

Whatever method a composer uses, however, he soon discovers that there are basic verities in Hollywood's use of music that he has to respect. Except in the rarest instances (so rare that I can hardly think of one off-hand) the music that is written for movies in Hollywood is channeled into certain well-defined categories—those that I mentioned at the outset of this chapter. There are "main titles" and "end titles," "montages" and "inserts"—and practically nothing else except background noises and atmospheric effects.

"Main titles" is Hollywood jargon for everything that happens before the movie actually starts—that is, the music that accompanies the "cards" or "titles" which announce the name of the picture, the credits for direction, action, script, lighting, sound and costumes. In musical films the problem is easily solved by merely scoring the important song for a heavy orchestra and playing it over several times.

However, for dramatic films the undertaking is rather more complex, for there has grown up a tradition of a big "sweep" for the opening. This is supposed to give an aura of impressiveness to the beginning of the film, even if you have already sat through half the picture and decided that it's lousy. "Sweep," in musical terms, implies a harp glissando, ascending-scale passages for the violins—*ff*—as well as for the woodwinds, all topped by a cymbal crash on the first beat, after which, grandiose tuttis. Steiner's "Mickey-Mouse" technique prompts him to write different music for each of the separate credit "cards." Newman, on the other hand, works for the mood of the whole picture, substantially disregarding the changes.

On the other hand, "montages" occur in the middle of the picture, generally in what I would describe as a "Vorkapich mood" (in tribute to Slavko Vorkapich, the technician who introduced this technique to Hollywood). These are the mixed-up sequences in which a variety of different scenes are flashed on the screen, sometimes superimposed on each other, to cover a lapse of time by allusions to incidents not described in the script. A favorite subject for the "Vorkapich mood" is honeymoons, in which a boat is seen pulling out of New York harbor, then there is a shot of the Savoy in London, the Champs Elysées in Paris, the pigeons at St Peter's in Rome and finally the Statue of Liberty. In this way the Will Hays office is appeased, and the audience is given to understand that a marriage has been consummated.

For some reason, the Paris music—with the boulevard in the background, the trees, Parisians sitting at
café tables—is always based on the walking music
from Gershwin's "American in Paris." This has become the standard thing, and any deviation from it
is looked upon with disdain by the producers. To a
certain extent this is understandable. However, when
the couple comes back to New York and the cab
drives up Broadway—*again* it is the "American in
Paris," with the same snappy one-step, the taxi horns
and the hustle bustle. On sunny days London is
similarly depicted, but this is a rarity in the films,
where the Strand is permanently enveloped in fog.

One of the most remarkable montages I ever saw
was in a picture with Jeanette MacDonald, in which
she played the part of a prima donna. The purpose of
this montage was to bridge over her transition from
obscurity to world celebrity, and it was done by a
series of superimposed opera bills, showing MacDonald singing at Monte Carlo, Paris, Berlin, Budapest,
Covent Garden and finally, of course, at the Metropolitan. The astonishing thing about this montage was
that the musical background contained themes from
Tristan and *Aïda*, *Traviata* and *Der Rosenkavalier*,
Il Barbiere di Siviglia and *Don Giovanni*—suggesting

[136]

that MacDonald could sing anything from Isolde to Violetta, from Rosina to Donna Anna. Even in the movies that is considerable territory.

Then there are "inserts," which are usually concerned with newspaper headlines announcing that District Attorney Huey is going to prosecute "Big Nose" Salvatore, leader of the dope ring in Steeltown. It has become established that frenetic Rimsky-Korsakoff trumpets, playing repeated seconds, are the precise thing for inserts of this sort. On the other hand, in mass processional scenes of the "Little Caesar" era, when a newspaper came hurtling out of the corner of the screen and you dimly saw an expensive funeral making its way down the street, you were certain to hear one of two things—either the "Dead March" from "Saul" (Handel) or the Funeral March from Chopin's B minor sonata. Warner's, I believe, was more partial to Chopin, while Fox and Universal went in more for the classic Handel.

In addition to these several specific categories (which permit of few variations) there are several species of fog music which deserve a word of attention. Ordinary fogs, such as those which hang over the English downs or the harbor at Calais, are invariably Ravel-Debussy, with the element of the latter derived from his "Fêtes" (the muted trumpets). However, special kinds of fogs, for prison breaks or bank robberies, require a certain admixture of horror. A few of the recondite figurations from Dukas's "L'Apprenti Sorcier" will satisfy this requirement very successfully.

I directed attention earlier to the specialized influence of music by Frederick Delius. As well as supplying backgrounds for walks in the garden, his music has proved exceptionally useful for the bicycle rides in the country that the daughter of the prime minister (English) takes with the leader of the Black and Tans (Irish) in Sinn Fein pictures, before she discovers that he is one of "those" people.

For some reason there is a tradition of train music in movies that has produced few examples of less than brilliant quality. Perhaps the accessibility of Honegger's "Pacific 231"—which settled this problem once and for all—has something to do with it. However, as early as the "Blue Horizon" number from *Monte Carlo* (the Lubitsch film with MacDonald and Jack Buchanan) there was a distinguished train episode. One of the best suggestive sequences of this sort was done by Stothart for the suicide scene in *Anna Karenina* with Garbo.

If there is a problem of anything roguish or slightly

unconventional in humor the bassoon will take care of it. If Richard Strauss has not collected any movie royalties for his "Til Eulenspiegel," it is not because his music has not been used in the films but merely because it has been signed by a variety of different names. It is, in fact, wearing a bit thin now, suggesting either that Strauss will have to write a new tone poem in the same vein or else the boys will have to find something else to be "generic" with.

The orchestral pattern of all carousels, incidentally, is derived from Stravinsky's "Petrouchka."

Speaking of Strauss brings to mind another type of musical film, in which two of the bit players are always the Emperor Franz Josef and Johann Strauss. My guess is that Franz Josef must have had a family of at least 2,000, for in each of these films he is in love with a different chorus girl or ballerina. As for the Strausses, senior and junior, they have quarreled and patched up more times even than James Stewart and Margaret Sullavan. This has been going on for years with only one predictable result—the picture is never a success.

It is these things that I had in mind at the outset of this chapter when I said that little attention is paid to the character of a score as a whole in Hollywood.

Obviously it is impossible for a composer to assert his individuality when everything he writes must fit into a predetermined space, when he is aware that there must be no nonsense of allowing an idea to develop.

I recognize that the limitations I have referred to from time to time are in the main due to the exigencies of the way pictures are produced. But such details as the lush orchestration, the constant use of musical clichés, the undeviating devotion to formulas are not to be excused on this basis.

It is a rather significant thing, I think, that no well-known American composer has ever been granted an opportunity by a Hollywood producer actually to assimilate the technique of writing for the films. If by some circumstance he is engaged for such a job—as, say, Hageman and Gruenberg have—he soon becomes aware that the requirements of the movies are quite different from those with which he is accustomed to work. The usual procedure is to make use of the material he writes—for the prestige value of his name—extensively reorganized by a specialist, usually an orchestrator. Then he is paid off, with no further chance to increase his experience or make use of what he has learned.

For it must be apparent by now that the large majority of scores used in Hollywood is written by specialists, and that there is pretty much of a closed shop for the specialists. All this results in a vicious circle in which the talented men do not have the experience, and the experienced men—largely speaking —have no particular talent. Thus the same clichés are repeated over and over in the same lush tradition of over-orchestrating.

It has always seemed a paradoxical thing to me that movie orchestration is practically the only movie activity in which there has been no retrenchment during the depression. There is still the conviction in Hollywood that a bloated tutti, with horns, trombones and cellos playing a melodic phrase, is the quickest way to the heart of the audience. No violins ever play in unison—only in sixths and thirds. Each episode, no matter what the implications of the scene, must be lined with orchestral gold and silver, with the horn figures inside, the clarinets and flutes on top, the ground swell of cellos and basses underneath.

I recall a Russian picture with a score by Shostakovitch which began with a single piccolo playing faintly in a high register. Then another woodwind entered, and the two voices were developed contrapuntally. This had ten times the personality of *all* the "main-title" music produced in Hollywood last year, with all its big "sweep." If a composer in Hollywood appeared at a studio with an opening sequence scored for one, three or five instruments the producer would think that he was not getting a proper return for his investment.

Nevertheless, Arthur Honegger wrote a fine movie score for the English *Pygmalion*, in which there was much writing for single instruments and, frequently, a lean, precise, economic kind of orchestration. He also achieved an excellent effect in his score for *Mayerling* with a small orchestra. Nor is this by any means a recent development in European writing for the movies. At least ten years ago Georges Auric wrote one of the best movie scores of all time for René Clair's *A Nous la Liberté*. It was witty without being self-conscious, fresh without being eccentric, terse without being sparse—and all done with a small orchestra.

As for Shostakovitch and Prokofieff, they have both done distinguished work for the films. Of the former I have already spoken. Prokofieff's entertaining score for *The Czar Sleeps* was good enough to be separated from its scenario and converted into a concert suite which has been played extensively by Koussevitzky and others as "Lieutenant Kije." I should not be surprised if there should be a similar development in the instance of his score for *Alexander Nevsky* (first heard in America with the film a year ago) which reveals a new aspect of Prokofieff's talent in its suggestions of Moussorgsky and Borodin. It is certainly unthinkable that an American composer should be allowed to reveal anything significant about himself, new or old, in a score he would write for Hollywood.

It is hardly believable that in so short a time the producers and their categories of writing for the screen should have become so firmly entrenched. However, this is precisely what makes the outlook so black. The patterns have been established by men who have no particular originality, and they must be respected by everyone who comes to Hollywood, regardless of what talents they may possess. Despite the vast quantities of music that are written in Hollywood each year, none of it is ever heard in the concert halls. On the other hand the men whose music is played in the concert hall rarely write for Hollywood.

Among persons of musical discrimination the only scores for American films that are spoken of with enthusiasm were written without exception for noncommercial films. I think particularly of Virgil Thomson's scores for *The Plow That Broke the Plains* and *The River*, both produced by the government. In the latter Thomson used mostly folk songs, and even a banjo. It was scored for a small group of musicians from the Philharmonic conducted by Alexander Smallens. I don't know whether Thomson was required by a budget to use a small orchestra; but I do know that it placed a premium on ingenuity, of which he has no lack.

Aaron Copland also did a distinguished job recently for *The City*, a film produced by the New York Housing Commission. It had point, atmosphere and appositeness—all without sacrificing musical quality. One of the most enjoyable musical experiences I have had was in directing the recording of the score written by the German Hanns Eisler for an animated film exhibited at the New York World's Fair. Not only was there pleasure in the brightness and clarity of his ideas, there was also distinction in the clean precision of his orchestration, the polish and finesse of his writing.

Of course, these men did not draw pay checks in five figures for their services. But, on the other hand, they did not have to run a gauntlet of producers, supervisors and "musical directors."

My Life

My Life

OR THE STORY OF GEORGE GERSHWIN

LONG BEFORE I EVER MET GEORGE Gershwin, or even heard of him, he had begun to impinge on my life. Like the first theme in an elaborate rondo, his was a discomfittingly insistent motive constantly recurring in my orbit, eventually to reduce me from industry to inertia.

Curiously, my first recollection of the theater was not at the age of four, being carried across the stage in the arms of Lillian Russell. (If anything, it was my secret desire at that time to carry her across the stage in my arms.) It was as a gallery spectator of a show called *Ladies First,* starring Nora Bayes. I was present of necessity, in tribute to my uncle Oscar Radin, who conducted the pit orchestra.

I don't remember a thing about the performance (this was around 1918, when I was about 12) except that in the second act the show stopped, Bayes came down front and did what amounted to her vaudeville turn. For those who don't remember, her singing was marked by a highly personal treatment of the music and words, in which the piano accompaniments played a very subtle and important part requiring almost constant improvisation.

After one chorus of the first song my attention left Bayes and remained fixed on the playing of the pianist. I had never heard such fresh, brisk, unstudied, completely free and inventive playing—all within a consistent frame that set off her singing perfectly.

Later when I reminded George of the show and his part in it he remarked that Bayes was constantly complaining that his playing distracted her from what she was trying to do, and that she frequently threatened to get somebody else.

When I was fifteen years old I left Pittsburgh, having realized that my chances of making the *Pirates* was something less than ephemeral. (My legs had gone bad.) Ever resourceful, however—this was pre-WPA —I returned to the piano as my instrument of vengeance.

Thus were established the two characteristics I have nurtured ever since as the dominating influences of my life—jealousy and revenge.

At this time musical life in New York was in a slothful, degenerate, sybaritic, undiscriminating, post-war hysteria of enthusiasm for such pianists as Paderewski, Rachmaninoff, Hofmann and Rosenthal—the public was content to be entertained rather than disturbed. Consequently, even though my scales were like a neurotic string of pearls, and my octaves, like the fabulous Zuleika Dobson "had no hips at all," I was forced to play dance music.

Since I had been orientated to a different musical background I had an unhealthy contempt for most of the tunes we played. They possessed no qualities on which my jealousy-revenge hunger could feed, being completely lacking in any enviable worth. Soon, however, I began to notice a few songs which had merit to arouse my resentment—"Do It Again," "I'll Build a Stairway to Paradise" and several others. Here, I thought, was something worthy of envy. I took note

[149]

of the composer's name—George Gershwin—a contemporary worthy of my most zealous dislike.

The thunderous shadow of George next cast its
light, paradoxically enough, on me with the febrile
tornado of the "Rhapsody in Blue." This transformed
my ivory tower of indifference to saxophone players
and drummers into a cyclone cellar, where I retreated
from his superiority.

However, my resentment fed quietly on itself until
after I had recorded the "Rhapsody" with Frank
Black for Brunswick early in 1925. He called me down
to the studio one morning when the regular pianist
failed to show up. Here was Black, helpless, with an
orchestra on his hands, wax waiting to be scarred and
indented—but it was an example of my business acu-
men that I went directly to the piano without making
a deal on the price for the job. When I was halfway
through the recording, having spared them the cost
of a rehearsal, it occurred to me they could pay me
whatever they wanted for the job, even union scale.
Which they did.

This, I reflected later, would not have happened
had I not been so fond of the music and so eager to
make the recording. I thought there might be consolation in a word of praise from the composer and called

him up "just to get his reaction," but mostly for approbation. I didn't get much.

Contrary to the common impression that composers do not think highly of their own ability as performers, Gershwin was quite firm in his preference for his own version on Victor. At this distance I can acknowledge that it is much superior.

It was after this that I began to make frequent unprofitable appearances on the radio, an industry which had a questionable future at the time and has since completely justified my uncannily prophetic knack. There was a thought in my mind that I might build up a following as a pianist in this way, but since I was never asked to play anything but the "Rhapsody" I merely increased its vogue and added to my reputation as a mono-pianist.

After my fourth appearance as soloist in the "Rhapsody" my mother wrote me a brief note, subtly suggesting that there were other works for piano and orchestra. She also expressed a hope that she might sometime hear me play on an important program like the Atwater-Kent or Roxy hour.

Shortly after this I was able to fulfill her desire, appearing as soloist with Rapee on the Roxy Broadcast. When I called her up after the broadcast she remarked not too cryptically,

"Again the 'Rhapsody!' "

My joy at hearing that Gershwin had been commissioned by the New York Symphony (now extinct, a victim of hardening of the tempi) to write a concerto could hardly have been exceeded by his—for now I would have another piece to play. Automatically my repertoire would be doubled. Thus I had more than ordinary interest in the progress of its composition—an interest which the late Thorstein Veblen, eminent economic strip-teaser, would have interpreted as not wholly sentimental in origin.

At this time my fortune took no turn, either for better or worse, because I had come under the aegis of the repetitive raconteur and genial maestro Ben Bernie (whose lust for ennui is his real metier—or is it horses?). I was pianist in his band and co-protégé (at the usual Bernie rates) with Phil Charig, the songwriter. He aspired to write shows and was serving the customary apprenticeship in the *École du Erlanger*, as rehearsal pianist for the Gershwin musicals of that season, *Tell Me More* and *Lady Be Good*.

I had often thought to myself, when I heard a new song by Gershwin, "Are our relations to remain for-

ever on the Tschaikowsky-Frau von Meck plane?"
Finally I beseeched Charig to effect an introduction
for me. There was a growing concern in my mind
about the progress of the work in which I had so definite a personal interest.

To my astonishment I found Gershwin amazingly
accessible at his apartment on 110th Street. When I
arrived he was working on the first movement of
"our" concerto with the late Bill Daly, his devoted
friend and favorite conductor. I had scarcely accustomed myself to the reality of his presence when I
realized that he was halfway through playing the new
work.

I was bristling with inarticulateness and stammered
some graceless remark.

George mistook my confusion and admiration for
disapproval, which in turn made him involuntarily
hostile. In addition to the work itself, his swift and
mettlesome piano playing had so stimulated and
excited me that the old dormant envy was reborn.

He was merely annoyed and returned to his work.
I left, having successfully made my usual bad impression.

However, when the work had its first performance
in Carnegie Hall I left Ben Bernie in the middle of

one of his bad jokes and found that my esteem for the work and his playing had not been vitiated by our angular meeting.

There followed an interim in which I began to write songs myself, some of them fairly successful. This led to a two-year hegira at very good money in Hollywood, following which I returned to Broadway to write a show for Fred Stone. I had begun to emerge somewhat from the Gershwin shadow in those years, recognizing him now not merely as a subject for an aesthetic envy, but, in my youthful bumptiousness, as a business competitor.

By coincidence, *Ripples*—the Stone show—was housed in the New Amsterdam Theater, geographically opposed to Gershwin's *Strike Up the Band* at the Selwyn. This juxtaposition renewed my old contrapuntal relationship with George, this time with the more brassy timbre contributed by our mutual interest in a chorus girl in his show ("Allegro Scherzando," song form ABA, with the second subject in the bass).

In addition to the ponderable advantage that accrued to him through the circumstance that his name was Gershwin and mine wasn't, he had the extra weight pull of a ducal fur-trimmed overcoat (known in the Kretchma set as a "peltz"). This was in his post-

Chotzinoff* period, giving him the appearance of a perpetual guest conductor.

In my favor were a slovenly appearance, a certain rudeness and a facility for creating anti-Gershwin propaganda ("conceited, big-headed." "Conceited, Big-headed." "CONCEITED, BIG-HEADED.") My tactics, in toto, were to appeal to the mother instinct latent even in a chorus girl as a social misfit, an irresponsible lad, an example of talent wasting for want of the proper guidance. I kept hinting that these veins could be tapped by the right woman, that I could go far with the proper girl. (I might go even farther with the wrong girl.)

For her part, she was devoted to *La Bohéme*, swooning in ecstasy with each saccharine cadence. George had difficulty in playing the Puccini score for her on the piano for two reasons: (A) It wasn't by Gershwin. (B) He didn't read other people's music very well (at that time).

It was, however, no problem for me, and I eventually found myself hoisted by my own petard, dripping Bohemians from each ear. But despite my fluency, the race was not to the swift. There was an element of wish fulfillment in her partiality for George, I always

*A music critic, and one of the early admirers of Gershwin's concert-hall works.

[155]

felt, his fur collar an association with Mimi's muff, which she always coveted.

During this mutually successful contretemps I also acquired a fondness for the score of *Strike Up the Band*. Even in those early days I had developed a facility for not being invited any place. Consequently most of my evenings were spent at the New Amsterdam Theater. As quickly as the score of *Ripples* palled on my audience, it palled on me more. Hypnotically, I would find myself at the rear of the Selwyn, resentfully transported by the fresh rhythms and humors of the Gershwin lyrics and music.

Ironically, it was just as I had my first musical show produced that George emerged with a wholly new concept of musical-comedy writing. Up until this time his librettos had not encouraged any departure from the clichés of boy-meets-girl songs. For the first time he was provided by George S. Kaufman and Morrie Ryskind with a book whose wry satiric wit illuminated a new facet of Gershwin's talent.

While in the spell of this discovery one afternoon I was tapped on the shoulder by a wraithlike figure asking,

"How is your show doing?"

This unmaliciously intended query returned me to

[156]

the banal reality of my own enterprise. At the conclusion of the act I, in turn, invited the shadowy inquirer to partake of my Jello-like score, having discovered that she was Leonore Gershwin, Ira's wife, whom I had met once before.

After she had seen a few numbers of *Ripples* she developed in me a scorn for my own music almost equal to hers. (The Stone show, I might add, was based on a fairy tale, which—contrary to vengeful whispers—is not my *genre*.) Like a missionary after office hours she led me back, symbolically, to the Selwyn, where I remained in spirit for the next nine or ten years.

She suggested that perhaps I would like to spend the evening with George and Ira, and I escorted her back to the apartment house on Riverside Drive, where the Gershwins occupied adjoining penthouses. These were connected by a short passageway that facilitated their work together and also the mutual interchange of guests. The house was mostly filled with an element of parasites, both aesthetic and gustatory. Here I discovered I was a born leader, for I soon took charge of this hitherto disorganized group.

Leonore was a gracious hostess and the first person to tolerate my unresolved social dissonances. With this encouragement, I flowered as a buffoon, warmed in the sun of this amiable household. I responded particularly to the friendship and tolerance of Leonore, spending hours and days in Ira's apartment. In fact, I once accused Ira of being in love with Leonore, and, like a guilty man, he blanched. I never referred to the subject again.

From the first day's supper I worked up to having four and five meals a day with the Gershwins, eating my way through the composition of the music and lyrics for *Delicious* and *Girl Crazy*. Out of sheer perverseness, I felt, George would cajole me frequently to leave the wonderful savory dishes on Ira's table to share with him a menu suited to his favorite ailment—"composer's stomach." It consisted of gruel (and such variants as oatmeal and farina) rusk, zwiebach, melba toast (only on festive occasions), Ry-krisp, Swedish bread and rusk. The *pièce de résistance* was stewed fruit or, when he was in a gluttonous mood, apple sauce.

Between the two households I emerged as a penthouse beachcomber. The two pianos in George's apartment made it possible for us to play his music together as it was written, for it was his custom to sketch his large works for two pianos before scoring them. The

"Second Rhapsody" and the "Cuban Overture" were written in this way and played over by us before assuming their final form.

Surrounding the music in the two apartments (Ira had a fondness for singing George's settings of his lyrics) both from the pianos and the phonographs, was a sporadic stream of talk embracing prize fighting, music, painting, football and sex. The Gershwin enthusiasm for ping-pong was communicated to me along with the scores, and we spent hours at the game. Amid this constant activity there was recurrently a recess for food, variously disguised as lunch, dinner, supper or midnight snack.

One such festival began with a midday bite in Ira's apartment and proceeded with the clock from one ménage to the other, with the invariable variety in entertainment, conversation and food. As the night progressed my endurance almost exceeded the politeness of my hosts. Eventually at six in the morning, when the conversation had for hours been sustained only by my garrulity, we found ourselves back in Ira's apartment. Leonore, Ira and George were ineffectively masking yawns when I returned from the icebox with part of an apple in my hand and the rest in my mouth and mumbled, "Pardon me for eating and running."

Once I had been admitted to George's friendship I took so much pleasure in the things he was writing and doing that I did nothing of my own. I got so much, vicariously, out of his ability and creativeness that whatever latent talents I had were completely submerged. In consequence I had no formative period as a composer. Listening to him improvise and play was enough for me. He had such fluency at the piano and so steady a surge of ideas that any time he sat down just to amuse himself something came of it. Actually this is how he got most of his ideas—just by playing. He enjoyed writing so much because, in a sense, it was play for him—the thing he liked to do more than anything else.

About this time he had started to collect paintings and simultaneously to develop his own considerable gift for painting. Between his own work and the paintings he had acquired by purchase the accumulation covered the walls of several rooms. Each stray, less-than-*femme-fatale* visitor would be escorted on a tour of the collection, accompanied by verbal annotations that eventually, through repetition, assumed the character of a guide's lecture. Included in his earliest acquisitions were a Modligiani, a Derain and a Roualt, the last of these one of his celebrated "Clowns." My insensitivity to painting was such that I once told George that no matter what he hung in their places there would still be a Modligiani and a Derain. The only one I would miss was the Roualt, for which I had a friendly feeling based on personal identification.

Among Gershwin's most ambitious efforts was a self-portrait in tails and high hat, which he modeled by a contrivance of mirrors. The arrangement was so elaborate and complicated that the painting gave the illusion of four Gershwins instead of one. In addition, the face itself conveyed the impression that Gershwin was covertly looking at himself out of the corner of his eye as he painted.

It is possible that his interest in painting was stimulated by a member of the family, to whom Gershwin always referred as "my cousin Botkin, the painter." While Botkin was abroad one summer with his usual commission to make purchases for George's collection —at a price—he discovered an obscure Picasso and had it shipped to New York. It was hung amid much ceremony, providing a welcome new subject for Gershwin's explanatory comment, as an example of Picasso's "blue period."

However, when George discovered that no catalogue of Picasso's work listed his "Absinthe Drinker," he began to ponder the shrewdness of Botkin's purchase. At length he had the picture photographed and sent a copy to Picasso in Paris, with a note of inquiry. Weeks passed without an answer, during which I had private pleasure in adding to his guided tours of the paintings that the Picasso had not been authenticated—to George's considerable irritation. At length another photo was dispatched, and this finally was returned with the scrawled superscription: This is my picture. Pablo Picasso.

This incident subsequently became a favorite footnote to George's expository comment on his paintings. It vanished, however, after the occasion on which he related the experience to a widely uncelebrated nightclub singer visiting the apartment. He happened to ruminate on the length of time it had taken Picasso to answer his query, and the girl suggested, "Perhaps he thought you were only trying to get his autograph."

The versatility of George's talents and the skill with which they were administered inspired patronizing comment from some of his worst admirers and allegedly best friends. This was reflected in an article by the ex-writer, *agent provocateur* for dross and actor, Alexander Woollcott, in *Cosmopolitan*. Since the unamiable Woollcott had no intimate knowledge either of modern music or painting, his capacity to deal with Gershwin judiciously was evident. My irritation with this article was conveyed to Woollcott when we chanced to meet a little later. Armed with indignation as well as loyalty, I insisted that he was qualified only to comment on Gershwin's personality —to which he retorted,

"Arguing with you is like fighting a man with three hands."

This remark, in the middle of our argument, pleased me and put me temporarily under his spell.

As well as collaborating with George in private performances of his music, I also had the opportunity occasionally to play his works in public. Incidentally, I had rehearsed his one-act opera *135th Street* several years before when Whiteman was preparing it for a concert. Our first association was in the summer of 1931, when the Stadium presented an all-American program in which Gershwin played the "Rhapsody" and I joined Robert Russell Bennett in a performance of his "March" for two pianos and orchestra. By coincidence the concert was postponed daily for almost a week because of rain. Each afternoon we would dress and have dinner together and then find that the concert was canceled again by an evening shower. This continued for five days, during which I received the only gratuitous publicity of my musical career, as the newspapers reprinted the program each day. By this time I almost regretted the arrival of a clear day, for playing became an anticlimax to my most active season as a soloist.

In the following summer the Stadium resumed its custom of presenting an all-Gershwin concert, and he flattered me by suggesting that I play the "Concerto." This was conditioned by the fact that he was playing both the "Rhapsody in Blue" and the "Second Rhapsody" and finally decided that he could not undertake the "Concerto," also. Six months before this I had made a feeble effort to escape the Gershwin thrall by getting married; but the success of this effort may be gauged by my action on the January day of the nuptials. It chanced that Leonore, Ira and George were leaving for Quebec for the winter sports (consisting of skiing and playing Canadian pianos) and I left my bride-to-be to see them off from the Grand Central Station.

As a result of my marriage, when I was hastily preparing the "Concerto" for the Stadium, I was living in an apartment house for the only time during the fifteen years of my residence in New York. (As a hotel dweller I had acquired an imperishable respect for the maternal instincts of bellboys and elevator operators.) My system was to work at each movement intensively until I had memorized it and then proceed to the next. I had at length mastered the first movement and was beginning my study of the second when a pianist in an apartment across the court from me started to memorize the first movement of—the Gershwin "Concerto." This was my first experience with musical sabotage, a kind of tonal boring from within.

The pleasure I had in appearing on the program with George was only exceeded by the little unpremeditated expressions of his reactions to the concert. It was hardly over when one of his truly well-disposed friends rushed back, wrung his hand and said,

"George, it was wonderful!"

"That's all?" said George, with characteristic abstraction. "Just wonderful?"

The friend was in turn followed by others, plus a considerable accumulation of autograph collectors. A cluster of talking, crowding persons marked the spot where Gershwin stood. Off at one side, with not even one of George's myriad second cousins, was

I. At length, disturbed and a little embarrassed, I edged around to the back of the group and said,

"You could send at least one of them over to me."

His reply was the generous offer to send over his younger brother Arthur.

However, he did repay me with a warming and disarming gesture a few days later. I came up to the apartment, and he greeted me with a small-boy smile, his hands clasped behind his back,

"What would you rather have," he said, "money or a watch?"—simultaneously handing me a handsome wrist watch inscribed with an affecting simplicity:

From George to Oscar
Lewisohn Stadium
August 15, 1932

It is by this watch that I have been late for every important appointment since then. But I'm grateful now that I didn't get what I would have preferred then—the money.

These successive Stadium concerts were always singular events in Gershwin's year, marking as they did a contact with a larger audience than he ever experienced elsewhere. It was also an inexpressible satisfaction for George to hear his music played by such an orchestra as the Philharmonic. Due, perhaps, to his background in a field—the commercial theater —where audience interest is the criterion of success (hence worth) he was keenly conscious of the drawing power of the all-Gershwin programs—not merely as a prop to his ego, but more particularly as a confirmation of the quality of his work.

I was not present at the concert in 1936, which, unforeseeably, was the last in which he participated. He was scheduled to leave immediately afterward for Hollywood to start work on a film. I had preceded him there on a commission of my own by several weeks.

However, a friend relates that the evening of the concert chanced to coincide with the hottest day of an unbearably hot New York summer. Actually, it was that day in late July on which was recorded the highest temperature in the city's history: 102.2°. Despite the oppressive heat that lingered after sundown a large crowd appeared for the concert at which George both conducted and played.

During the intermission the friend wandered backstage to exchange a greeting with George, to find him in conversation with Mrs Charles Guggenheimer, director of the Stadium concerts. She was exuding

[167]

enthusiasm for the performance, but George seemed detached and inattentive.

When she paused for a moment he said,

"How's the crowd?"

"Grand," she answered. "More than twelve thousand."

With a shake of his head, Gershwin observed, "Last year we had seventeen thousand."

The friend interrupted, "Don't forget, George—this was the hottest day in the history of New York."

He brightened a little at this and remarked, with that curious mixture of irrelevance and seriousness, "That's right. I know four friends of mine who were supposed to come, but they were overcome by the heat."

It was through my professional association with George that I made my re-entry into Pittsburgh musical life. This was in 1934, when Gershwin was invited to play the "Rhapsody" and "Concerto" with the orchestra there. Bill Daly was scheduled to conduct, but he couldn't leave New York in time to do the rehearsal the day before the concert. So George suggested that I come out with him and play the solo parts while he got the orchestra in shape.

At that time I was acting as court pianist, at a

distance of six thousand miles, to Admiral Byrd, who was conducting researches into solitude in the Antarctic at "Little America." Each Saturday night the Grape Nuts Orchestra, which Daly conducted, would broadcast good cheer, to which the explorers responded by singing back at us sea chanteys and barroom ballads with slightly frigid intonations.

It was thus at the sacrifice of my honorary position in this orchestra that I accompanied George to Pittsburgh to make my triumphal return to my native city —and my only appearance there in a concert hall—in a rehearsal.

We took a late train for the overnight trip, sharing a drawing room. A lengthy discussion of music occupied us for an hour or so, and I was actually in the midst of answering one of his questions when he calmly removed his clothes and eased himself into the lower berth with the proprietary air befitting a member of one of Lundberg's *Sixty Families*.

There was nothing left for me to do but undress and attempt to finish my sentence as I did. George, however, resumed the thread of his discourse, and I suggested perhaps it was difficult for him to sleep on a train and would he like one of my sleeping pills—

with the air of a man offering a friend an after-dinner mint.

I adjusted myself to the inconveniences of the upper berth, reflecting on the artistic-economic progression by which Paderewski has a private car, Gershwin a drawing room and Levant a sleepless night. At this moment my light must have disturbed George's doze, for he opened his eyes, looked up at me and said drowsily, "Upper berth—lower berth. That's the difference between talent and genius."

This was characteristic of a certain undertone in our friendship, in which there was always a small element of nastiness, a fondness for putting the blast on each other. There was the occasion at a party several years later in which—as was the invariable consequence—an evening with Gershwin was a Gershwin evening. There were recurrent, lengthy references to his piano playing, his composing, his conducting, his painting —marcato monologues in alla breve which George's audience absorbed with the fascinated attentiveness of a Storm-trooper listening to one of Hitler's well-modulated firehouse chats.

Finally there was a *Luftpause*, and I inquired, "Tell me, George, if you had to do it all over, would you fall in love with yourself again?"

[170]

This discursiveness, however, was merely one manifestation of his desire to share with the world the
inexplicable phenomenon known as George. Another
was the extreme gregariousness of his nature, which
took the form of frequent parties in his home to com-
memorate almost any occurrence in his life. They also
served as diversion from his work and as a satisfaction
of his need, as a bachelor, for companionship. He had
a curious partiality for successful, well-to-do people
of the stockbroker type with whom he could play
golf and go on week ends, but there were always other
people around who were attracted by his enormous
vitality, the worth and genuineness of his accomplishments.

He was tremendously fond of being amused and of
making the contribution of his own healthy strain
of humor to the total of the banter. For months at a
time we would keep little inconsequential phrases
running, with no meaning for anyone but ourselves—
such as the story of my mother and the "Rhapsody."
Whenever somebody did something that he had done
or said twenty times before, our mutual comment was:

"Again the 'Rhapsody.' "

In the same way, his distrait "Just wonderful?"

became a catch phrase of incredulity for anything that merited admiration.

An important contribution to the sum of this humor was "Papa" Gershwin, whose unpredictable reactions to any situation, no matter how pat, supplied both Ira and George with an endless fund of stories. Physically his characteristics are more closely preserved in Ira than they were in George, but his gift for oblique thinking and apparently irrelevant simplicity was not unlike certain attitudes of George.

Pride in the accomplishments of his sons was an inseparable element of their father's life, with an occasionally remarkable consequence. Early in George's career he paid a business call to the office of Harms, his publishers, accompanied by "Papa." Gershwin had completed his business and was about to leave when Lou Hirsch, whose "Love Nest" was then the reigning hit, selling at a rate unknown in these days, emerged from an inner office with a check in his hands.

"Look at this," he exclaimed to George. "The first quarter's royalties—twenty-six thousand dollars."

George fingered the check and made some properly incredulous comment.

Then, feeling that "Papa" would enjoy a glimpse

of this historic document, he turned to him and said, "Hey, Pop—take a look at this check."

"Papa" took the check, considered its sum for a moment and handed it back to its owner. Seizing Hirsch's hand, he pumped it vigorously and said with brisk encouragement,

"Good luck, Mr Hirsch."

When the Gershwins ascended to the eminence of adjoining penthouses on West Seventy-fifth Street, after successive moves downtown from One Hundred Tenth to One Hundred Third Street, the décor of the apartments was responsive to the dominant tone of the day—so-called "modden." Severe lines, black and white furnishings, chromium ash trays and all the rest of the post Bel-Geddes innovations abounded in the two apartments, with special emphasis in George's.

A group of society women that George had acquired in his expanding career was being shown through the apartment one afternoon when "Papa" Gershwin appeared from an adjoining room and attached himself to the pilgrimage. George was called to the telephone, leaving the visitors engrossed in admiring comment and learned analysis of "functional lines," "expressive angles" and further exchange of catch phrases. "Papa" edged closer, and desiring to make some contribution to the sum of this temporal discussion, blandly inquired,

"Tell me, ladies—whatever became of 'Oh! fudge?' "

However, George's favorite "Papa" Gershwin story antedated any of these. It followed the opening of one of the first *Scandals*, for which George contributed a lengthy, brilliant and intensely original score. On the morning after the opening "Papa" came into the music room where George worked and expressed his particular preference for one of the songs in the show. There was no way in which he could identify it for George musically, and his whistling did not resolve the problem.

Finally the composer sat down at the piano, determined to discover his father's preference. Naturally he began with the hit song of the show, "Somebody Loves Me," and played sequentially all of the twenty numbers of the revue. Each one was rejected with a shake of the paternal head. In desperation, George began the progression again and had hardly played the first strain of "Somebody Loves Me" when "Papa" exclaimed,

"That's it—that's the one. Why didn't you play it the first time?"

No matter how much effort George had put into

the writing of a musical comedy or one of his orchestral scores, George never missed an opportunity to attend a rehearsal, ostensibly to do what might be necessary in pointing up the work, or to make a suggestion for the staging of a number, but really because he did not have the detachment toward his own work that is supposed to be a characteristic of composers. It was my ascetic contention that in writing something my creative impulse had asserted itself and I was not interested in the performance of the work. However, I was rarely put in the position of resisting temptation.

We went together to a rehearsal of the "Cuban Overture" (originally called simply "Rhumba") which George, with patriotic diplomacy, had written after a short trip to Havana. It was being prepared by Albert Coates for performance at the Stadium, and we arrived in the midst of an intricate rhythmic passage. Coates was concerned with unraveling the nosegay of percussive effects which George had tossed to our Southern neighbors, requiring the services of an extra group of players to augment the Philharmonic battery.

They were shaking gourds and maraccas, ahead and behind the beat, but with none of the precision or sharpness of accent that the patterns required, to Coates's considerable exasperation. He stopped several times to beat out the rhythm and correct the mistakes. Finally, when the passage still failed to go smoothly, he dropped his baton and delivered a scathing lecture on their incompetence.

One of the musicians patiently waited for Coates to conclude his discourse and then said (with an accent that would automatically have disqualified him from admittance to the Berlin Philharmonic), "Vee is Americans, Mr Coates—and here you is esking us to play Cuban rhythms."

Through his meeting, on his most recent jaunt to Europe, with such composers as Ravel, Stravinsky, Poulenc and Tansman, Gershwin had become aware of certain shortcomings in his equipment. There was no lack of admiration for his writing, but his lack of schooling with an acknowledged master put him in the position of a brilliant student from the East Side who entered Harvard from night school instead of by way of Groton. He once entertained thoughts of studying with Ravel, with whom he enjoyed very friendly relations, but after discovering traces of his own influence in Ravel's piano concerto I suggested that the results of such study might be retroactive.

However, in Joseph Schillinger, a theorist of Russian background living in New York, Gershwin found a musical analyst whose ideas and methods of procedure fascinated him. As much as anything else, he was attracted by Schillinger's reduction of all musical procedures, from the most formidable to the least imposing, to a mathematical system which he contracted to impart in a definite calendar period—a compositional equivalent of playing the piano in six easy lessons. Surprisingly enough this was thoroughly efficacious if taken with the considerable mixture of application that George contributed to the studies.

This was but one reflection of George's broadening horizon about this time. His curiosity about things, however, was translated into a curiosity about himself, a need for knowing himself better. He reasoned that having previously known himself only emotionally, he should also know himself scientifically, which immediately propelled him into psychoanalysis. This was a wholly unnecessary adventure, for it proved him to be enthusiastically unneurotic. However, during the year and a half of analysis it provided him with a fresh vein of after-dinner conversation, a laboratory variation, with clinical underscoring, on the theme of "Just wonderful?"

His enthusiasm about his two preoccupations at this time—Schillinger and psychoanalysis—had its reverberations in my life, for I, too, embarked on a course of study with Schillinger and also permitted myself to be psychoanalyzed. However, when George discovered that I had followed his suggestion in both instances he wrathfully accused me of jealousy, of imitating him.

All this was a slightly frenzied counterpoint to one of the most ambitious undertakings of his life—the writing of *Porgy*. There always seemed to me in this score a considerable evidence of his studies with Schillinger; not, of course, in the melodic writing or the songs, but in the working out of the rhythmic patterns, the planning of such episodes as the fugal background for the crap-game scene and in some of the choral passages. Schillinger's theories of cyclical harmonic progressions, with an intricate leading of bass notes, his scheme of rhythmic permutations, extended George's resources considerably.*

In consequence of his long absorption with *Porgy*, George was irresistibly drawn to the Guild Theatre

*Much of this theoretic practice can be found in the variations on "I Got Rhythm" (written for his tour with orchestra in 1934) and also in the interesting two-voice canon in the "Cuban Overture"—which has the unusual feature of being written against a full harmonic background, in contrast to most canons.

[178]

each day during the rehearsal period. In addition to his music, the theater boasted the congenial atmosphere contributed by two men—Rouben Mamoulian and Alexander Smallens—both experts in their field and sympathetic to Gershwin.

His presence on one occasion doubtless saved, for the audiences that subsequently enjoyed it, one of the great performances of *Porgy*—the "Sporting Life" of Bubbles. Gershwin shared the opinion of Fred Astaire (who studied Bubbles' dancing by the hour when Bubbles was an obscure hoofer in Harlem cafés) that the slim, dapper Negro was one of the great performers of the day and a dancer beyond compare. Moreover, he had personally scouted Bubbles for the part and shaped it to fit his talents.

Bubbles' negligence about rehearsals and promptness almost overbalanced his abilities, however; and on one occasion Smallens' exasperation with the absent Bubbles caused him to fling down his baton and shout to Mamoulian,

"I'm sick of this waiting. We'll have to throw him out and get somebody else."

Gershwin bounded from his seat a few rows back in the darkened theater and rushed down the aisle.

[179]

"Throw him out?" he said. "You can't do that. Why, he's—he's the black Toscanini!"

Since Bubbles could not read music his part had to be taught to him note by note. In ensemble passages and sections of complicated writing for the orchestra this inevitably led to difficulties about his entrances, note values and so on. Under the stress of successive repetitions of one scene, Smallens finally rose from his chair, slammed his fist on the score and shouted the correction to Bubbles. Then he proceeded to enumerate the times he had corrected Bubbles on this point and to inquire perhaps there was something at fault in his conducting.

Bubbles looked down contritely from the stage and said,

"Mr Smallens, if I had the money of the way you conduct I'd be a millionaire."

During this period my life reached the fullest flower of its aimlessness. This, in an obscure word, was my otiose period. Blooming with a deathlike glow, I had been lying fallow during the three long years in which *Porgy* was composed, sung, cast, rehearsed, discussed but never disparaged, relived and finally produced. From time to time I would appear at Gershwin's magnificent duplex on East Seventy-second Street, to find

George absorbed not only in the composition of *Porgy* but also in the manipulation of his extensive arsenal of writing equipment.

The desk in which it was housed, in his work-room, represented an incredible synthesis—in the pure Stokowskian sense of that term—of carpentry and composition. It consisted not merely of the usual flat-topped writing surfaces, but also of panels, drop leafs and other protruding appendages that made it possible for him to work without hunching over, in fact, almost without breathing. It had been made to his specifications and included racks for pens, drawers for rulers, triangles and T-squares, pigeonholes for erasers, pencils and sharpening-knives, built-in ash trays and a streamlined wastebasket. In fact, one absorbed the impression, in contemplating it, that in moments of extreme inspiration the desk would be psychically drawn to him.

For me, the most remarkable feature of the apartment was its ingenious design. A bachelor apartment of fourteen rooms, George had managed to devise a layout that omitted even a single guest room. I once confronted him with this insistence of exclusiveness, accusing him of foreseeing the occasion when I might want to stay over some night.

It is an interesting commentary on Gershwin's talent that despite its manifestation in half-a-dozen extended works he never wrote a score in a strict musical form. He could never accustom himself to such restraints as sonata form, or a fully developed rondo or any other of the classic molds. The thematic fluency, the easygoing rhythmic freedom of the rhapsody or unrestricted fantasy was his natural genre. One may carp for a slight exception in favor of the concerto, but it is the Lisztian mantle draped loosely on the skeleton of the sonata form. I never heard him consider, even conversationally, the writing of a symphony or any other work in such a clearly defined form.

To me this was a natural consequence of his training as a song writer and the conditioning it exerted on the treatment of the ideas that came to him. It was a stroke of remarkable good fortune that his serious consideration of such a play as Ansky's *Dybbuk* for operatic purposes was set aside in favor of *Porgy*, in which his song-writing talent found a natural outlet through his Negroid characters. Though such numbers as "Summertime," "It Ain't Necessarily So" and "I Got Plenty of Nuttin'," are songlike, they were more consciously composed than his usual musical-comedy numbers; and when *Porgy* was at length out of his hands the old desire to work in his first vein reasserted itself.

Then, too, once the fever of absorption in *Porgy* had been dispelled Gershwin became aware that such men as Cole Porter and Richard Rodgers had made a considerable advance into the territory once indisputably his. There was, of course, a considerable problem of adjustment, after the freedom of *Porgy*, to the more precise definitions of the popular song; but Gershwin nevertheless welcomed the opportunity when it presented itself—the assignment to write the score for *Shall We Dance*, with Astaire and Rogers.

Shortly before the Gershwins accepted this commission I had been engaged to write the opera which supplied the background for *Charlie Chan at the Opera*. This epic in abnormality brought together Warner Oland, as Chan, and Boris Karloff as a Mephistophelian Bing Crosby, for the first time in pictures. The producer's blind instinct, coupled with a limited budget, had sought me out to compose the opera.

Thus I was already in Hollywood when the Gershwins arrived early in August 1936. Among the ceremonies of greeting was a dinner party in their honor given by Edgar Selwyn, who had produced *Strike Up the Band*. This ceremonial dinner proceeded—after food and drink—to the piano, where George launched into a résumé of his music, old and new. Among the guests were Alexander Steinert, a Prix de Rome winner who had done considerable valuable work in the preparation of the chorus for *Porgy* and also conducted its road tour. In sheer politeness George finally suggested that Steinert play something of his own, in the confident belief that the surroundings and his own abashment would dissuade him. However, Steinert responded with the whole of a piano concerto by himself, which George slightly resented as an excess of acquiescence.

One of the reasons I accepted this Chan-Karloff commission was the opportunity it afforded me to resume studying with the great and provocative Arnold Schoenberg, whose influence had so deeply stimulated me a year and a half before. My appointments with him were on Tuesday and Friday mornings at an hour which required a heroic uprising on my part and exacted its inevitable toll. I had always resented sleep as an intrusion on my nocturnal self-pity, and the necessity of rising at eight in the morning merely re-duced from six to four the hours of tossing and sleep-lessness induced by sedatives.

The California sun beating down on my bulbous features brought to the surface all the accumulated poisons of my sedentary Eastern life—where my usual exercises consisted of groveling, brooding and mulling. An epic in bloat, I would proceed after my Schoen-bergian interlude to the Gershwins' for lunch, to be greeted by George as an unattractive reminder of Diego Rivera, for whom he had great admiration—as a painter.

George was greatly intrigued and faintly annoyed by the abstruseness of the music I was writing, so sharply different from his own. With a certain pride and even more aggression I displayed a completed piece one day, to which he responded, after an ex-amination,

"It looks so confused."

"Didn't you know?" I retorted. "I've just been of-fered the chair of confusion at U.C.L.A."

For George the manifold attractions of California provided the atmosphere for a ceaselessly active life, both physical and intellectual. A good many of the possibilities for outdoor activity were gathered into the back yard of the house—including a swimming pool, a tennis court and a ping-pong table. Interspersing his work on *Shall We Dance* with a session with one or another of these was a passion with George, but tennis was second in his interest only to the piano.

His pursuit of this sport permitted a transferral of the desk motive to the outdoors, represented by a dazzling array of shirts, shorts, slacks, shoes and a repertory of tropical beach robes of almost Oriental splendor. Unlike almost any other sport, tennis requires a grounding in technical form (Hear! Hear!) but George played good tennis almost by ear, and in contradiction of all known theories of foot position, swing or timing. His absorption in tennis was so complete that part of his man Paul's manifold duties was to volley with him in pre-game warm-ups.

Though George did not allow me on the court, he did not lack for competition. His brother Ira was as devoted to the game as he was, and the court was open to all their co-workers from New York domiciled in Hollywood. They would drop in almost daily for a game, a new Gershwin tune and a sandwich. With his concern for the sartorial aspects of tennis, George forbade me access to the court, since my tennis costume was identical with my costume for every other occasion—a dark, subtlely spotted business suit, suitable for all Farenheits from 0 to 212, heavy leather shoes, shirt and tie. I shared George's lack of form in my tennis and added to it my own lack of aptitude. Somehow I could not separate its objective from that of baseball, and the pop flies I batted over Beverly Hills could easily have been photographed for use as the locust holocaust in *Good Earth*.

Even exceeding George's passion for tennis was that of Schoenberg, who played with the scientific absorption of a man who wants to know what makes the ball tick (but not hit). The meeting of Schoenberg and Gershwin was an affectionate one and resulted, among other things, in a standing invitation for the older man to use the Gershwin court on a regular day each week. He would arrive with an entourage consisting of string-quartet players, conductors and disciples.

On one occasion, after playing two vigorous sets, Schoenberg and his opponents were driven from the court by a sudden shower, taking refuge in a shelter where George and I joined them. The sixty-odd-year-old Schoenberg wiped his brow and said, half to himself,

"Somehow I feel tired. I can't understand it."

Then added suddenly,

"That's right. I was up at five this morning. My wife gave birth to a boy."

"Why didn't you tell us before?" said George. "Come inside, we'll drink a toast."

We adjourned to the house, the glasses were filled, and George spoke touchingly of the event. As he was about to drink, George raised his glass and paused,

"Why don't you call him George? It's a lucky name."

Schoenberg shook his head wearily. "You're too late. I already have a son named George."

One of the most memorable experiences I have ever had in music occurred during that California visit, when Mrs Elizabeth Coolidge sponsored the performance of the four Schoenberg quartets and the last group of Beethoven, played by the Kolisch ensemble. George, Ira and I were overjoyed by this opportunity, and all of the music impressed us deeply.

We were all together on the tennis court one morning when the talk turned to the concert of the previous day.

"I'd like to write a quartet some day," said George. "But it will be something simple, like Mozart."

Schoenberg mistakenly interpreted Gershwin's typi-

cally irrelevant reflection as a comment on his work
and answered, somewhat nettled,

"I'm not a simple man—and, anyway, Mozart was
considered far from simple in his day."

Though George's acquaintance with formal music
was a rather scattered one he had pronounced likings
both in classic and contemporary works. A rather
curious discernment—since it was so opposed to the
characteristics of his own work—was his perception
of the quality in Alban Berg's music. He first became
acquainted with the "Lyrische Suite" by this most
famous of Schoenberg's pupils in 1927 during a visit to
Vienna. This, of course, was several years before Berg
was known even as a name in America. Gershwin
treasured the piano score of *Wozzeck* and was deeply
impressed by the opera when he journeyed to Philadelphia for the performance under Stokowski in 1931.

Like many another musician, George found that
he could get even more from phonograph records of
his favorite works than he could from their scattered
performances in public. Among the albums I recall
which gave him particular pleasure were Stravinsky's
"Symphonie des Psaumes," the first symphony of
Shostakovitch, the Milhaud violin concerto, the
"Lyrische Suite" of Berg and the complete Schoen-

berg quartets privately recorded by the Kolisches in
California. Somewhere, somehow, he had acquired a
liking for the records of Honegger's lively operetta
Les Aventures du Roi Pausole. On the other hand, he
admired greatly certain records of Duke Ellington's
orchestra for their rich effects and fine tonal originality—mood pieces like the "Creole Love Song,"
"Swanee Rhapsody" and "Daybreak Express."

Among modern works he studied in score were
Stravinsky's "Les Noces," the third piano concerto of
Prokofieff, the Debussy piano preludes—for which he
had great fondness—and various orchestral works by
this composer and Ravel. During the period of work
on *Porgy* he referred constantly to the score of *Die
Meistersinger* as a guide to the plotting of the choral
parts and for general precepts in vocal writing. Curiously, however, he refused throughout his career to
study orchestration with a teacher, preferring his
pragmatic approach, bulwarked by Cecil Forsyth's
Orchestration, which he regarded almost as a Bible.

We had our constant gags about "favorite" composers for the sake of mock interviews. As a satiric
commentary, they were invariably men with the most
grotesque names we could discover—such as César Cui,
Xavier Scharwenka (or was it Phillipe?) and as the

final crushing blow, Ed Poldini, composer of "Poupée Valsante." So far as a partiality in older music was concerned, however, George leaned particularly toward certain expansive moods of Brahms, whose string quartets we frequently played four-handed at the piano. It was the long line and free development of melodic material in Brahms that particularly attracted him. He also like the Mozart string quartets, which we played in four-hand versions.

As a corollary, he identified certain expressions of his own with this composer, referring to the second theme of the "Second Rhapsody"—a swelling legato subject in A major—as a "Brahms theme." Also, one of his last songs to be published, "Love Walked In," was always associated in his mind as a "Brahms strain." The idea for this had come to him some seven or eight years before it made a public appearance, but the difficulty of setting a lyric to it had delayed its completion until Ira's happy thought when the brothers were working on *Goldwyn Follies*.

One of his favorite chamber-music works was the great C major quintet (with two cellos) of Schubert, with which he first became acquainted during the period when he was writing *Of Thee I Sing* and *Let 'Em Eat Cake*. As a matter of fact, there is a slight influence of the beautiful second theme of the quintet's first movement in the tune he wrote for *Let 'Em Eat Cake* —"Two Hearts Are in Communion," in the "Union Square" number.

George played little concert music at the piano, with the exception of certain Chopin preludes, for which he had no pronounced interpretative feeling. For technical purposes, when he was preparing to play his own music in public, endless repetitions of the first Cramer study sufficed.

On the whole, the playing of his music by others found him an invariably approving and enthusiastic audience, and he would frequently express astonishment when I would make some critical comment on the flaws in this performance or that which we had heard together. There was one exception, however, when the concertmaster of the St Louis Symphony, playing "Summertime" as a violin solo during a potpourri from *Porgy*, followed the orchestra at the respectful distance of a bar during the whole piece, with excruciating results. George's strongest reaction was,

"You'd think anybody would know *that* tune!"

During his final visit to California he found an extremely sympathetic interpreter in Pierre Monteux, of the San Francisco Orchestra. Gershwin was thoroughly impressed with Monteux's excelling technical skill as a conductor, his exceptional rhythmic sensitivity and his amazing grasp—for a conductor of traditional background and alien nationality—of the spirit of Gershwin's music.

One of the most revealing remarks I ever heard George make on his own music occurred one afternoon in his apartment when we were playing over various scores, finally to arrive at something by Manuel de Falla. There had been some exchange of comment on "vertical" composers (those in which the interest in the music is primarily melodic) against so-called "horizontal" composers (in which the melodic interest is amplified by constant contrapuntal interchanges between the various voices). In the midst of playing the Falla score George stopped and said, with a slight touch of disparagement,

"He's a kind of Spanish Gershwin."

It was a particular source of pride for him that two movements of his piano concerto were included in the American program which Fritz Reiner conducted at the Venice International Festival of Contemporary Music in 1932. The work was well received, and the continuous applause prompted Reiner and Harry

Kaufman, who was the piano soloist, to repeat the finale.

This fact lingered in the back of Gershwin's mind, apparently, for in a casual conversation several years later a visitor mentioned that he had been present at that performance. George's interest in the conversation immediately sharpened.

"You were there?" he said. "Tell me about it. I never had a chance to speak to anybody who was actually there."

The visitor recalled his impressions of the occasion, cited the enthusiasm of the largely Italian audience and complimented Kaufman's playing. He added, of course, that the last movement had been repeated.

"They repeated the last movement," George echoed, as though hearing it for the first time.

Turning to another guest he said, "Think of that. The only other time in musical history it ever happened was when the Boston Symphony first gave the Tschaikowsky piano concerto in 1894."

No doubt his visitors were baffled by the elucidation of this odd, segregated bit of information, but George's reading on musical subjects was surprisingly wide and varied. In addition to such standard fact books as the Grove Dictionary and Cobbett's *Cyclopaedic*

Survey of Chamber Music, his library included virtually every worthwhile musical book of his own time, and many older ones. He once amazed me, in a discussion of folk songs and their permissibility in formal composition (my argument was that it was cheating for a composer to use ready-made material), by citing the first theme of Beethoven's "Pastoral" symphony as a Dutch folk song and producing the reference to prove it.

Despite this increasing interest in formal music and its background Gershwin never lost his love for dance music. The emergence of the swing phenomenon interested but did not surprise him, for such eminent performers as Benny Goodman, Gene Krupa, Red Nichols, Jack Teagarden, Jimmy Dorsey, Babe Rusin and Glenn Miller had contributed to the gayety of *Strike Up the Band* and *Girl Crazy* as members of the pit orchestra. The Goodman trio's record of "Lady Be Good" delighted him, and he listened with rapture to Art Tatum (the great blind Negro pianist), especially to his playing of "Liza" and "I Got Rhythm."

He was so enthused with Tatum's playing that he had an evening for him at his Seventy-second Street apartment before leaving for Hollywood. Among George's invited guests was Leopold Godowsky, who

listened with amazement for twenty minutes to Tatum's remarkable runs, embroideries, counter-figures
and passage playing. The succeeding hour and a half
of the same thing bored him, however. Some time
after he arrived in California Gershwin discovered
that Tatum was playing at a local night club, and we
went together to hear him. It was a small, dingy, badly
lighted room—an intimate version of the too-intimate
Onyx Club. We joined the group of enthusiasts clus-
tered around the piano where the blind virtuoso was
in full swing. To George's great joy, Tatum played
virtually the equivalent of Beethoven's thirty-two
variations on his tune "Liza." Then George asked for
more.

For one of the few occasions in my experience,
George was genuinely offended when the composition of the score for the *Goldwyn Follies* had
progressed almost to the point of completion. The
producer summoned him to a conference one afternoon and insisted that the performance of the music
be given in the presence of his full staff of loyal,
well-paid amanuenses (stooges). Being with justice
suspicious of his own opinion, Goldwyn augmented it
with an a cappella choir of enthusiasts. The experience
of thus submitting his work for the approbation of a

dummy panel, whose opinion was as predictable as the result of a Jersey City election, humiliated George —who felt that this stage of his career had long since passed.

His resiliency was attested by the amusement he derived on the following day when the story conferences began with Goldwyn and George Balanchine (choreographer, ballet master and husband of Vera Zorina). For the first time in his career Goldwyn found himself challenged in dialectics by Balanchine, whose own broken English was hardly less fragmentary than his employer's. It was veritably a "Great Waltz" of accents—in which, by some remarkable divination, they established a common meeting ground based on mutual incomprehensibility. The Gershwins, however, frequently felt themselves in need of an interpreter.

Balanchine, caught unaware at this conference, was improvising the scenario for his ballet in the film and stumbled across the word "competition" as the leitmotiv of a dance sequence involving some banal conflict of Jazz vs Classics.

"That's great," said Goldwyn, *"Competition!"*— lunging at the word as though he had at last encountered a compatible emotion.

[197]

It was during the period of work on the *Goldwyn Follies* that the first evidence of George's illness asserted itself. All during his residence in California he had devoted himself recurrently to making public appearances as a pianist, even in cities as remote as St Louis, Seattle, Portland and Detroit, making overnight trips by plane. One would see George on a certain day and return the next day to discover he was in the middle of a tour. This series culminated with his first appearance in Los Angeles, as soloist at a concert conducted by Smallens. The chorus and soloists of *Porgy and Bess* also appeared.

Though he had played the "Concerto" dozens of times in public with great fluency I noticed that he stumbled on a very easy passage in the first movement. Then, in the andante, in playing the four simple octaves that conclude the movement above the sustained orchestral chords, he blundered again. When I went backstage he greeted me with the curious remark,

"When I made those mistakes I was thinking of you, you . . . " concluding with some gruffly uncomplimentary characterization.

At the second concert of the series, on the following night, he afterward remarked that he had experienced a curious odor of some undefinable burning smell in his nostrils as he was conducting one number, and a sudden dizzy headache. Nobody considered it to be anything of moment, including George himself. He was so completely the personification of vitality and resonant health that a physical or mental breakdown seemed altogether unthinkable, particularly to George. The care of his physical being was almost a mania with him, a pursuit which he cultivated with considerable success. In the hills near his Hollywood home he had staked out a six-mile walk, whose daily execution seemed to me not only a feat in physical endurance but also an action traitorous to everything for which I stood.

I have no taste for annotating the next—and last—six months of George's life. There are, however, certain things which I would like to say briefly. The recurrence with increasing frequency of the headaches disturbed his friends, but not because they associated it with any organic disorder. The spells were interpreted as a neurotic manifestation of his dissatisfaction with working conditions in Hollywood, an expression of his yearning to be elsewhere.

This, however, was plainly fallacious, for George's interests at this time continued to expand, his work went well and his mental outlook was altogether healthy. He took a great interest in the contemporary music that was being played in Los Angeles at the time, where, contrary to the usual opinion, the musical atmosphere was a sharp and bracing one. Stravinsky made a guest appearance with the Los Angeles Orchestra, conducting his own works; there were the Schoenberg quartet concerts; the WPA Schoenberg-and-pupils concert; the presence of Ernest Toch and Aaron Copland on the coast—all these things interested and stimulated him.

The freshness of these contacts, indeed, aroused George to the contemplation of renewed work in large forms, which had not engaged his attention since *Porgy* more than two years before. From his conversation I believe this would have been in the field of ballet or, possibly, a string quartet.

As the weeks went on the headaches George suffered did not arouse anything more than quizzical comment until several months after their first occurrence, when a particularly severe attack prompted Leonore and Ira to insist that George submit to a thorough physical checkup.

This finally occurred on a Sunday morning, some six or seven weeks before his last Sunday. The doctor and neurologist arrived, and we went outside in the garden to have lunch. There was no ominous strain or tension in the air, for there had been no suspicion on which to base such feelings.

When George came down and shuffled over in his beach robe and sandals I called to him facetiously,

"What did the doctors say?"

He laughed, as in relief, and said,

"Well, before they told me anything they wanted to rule out the possibility of a brain tumor."

With this final irony—in retrospect as in actuality—I reject the association of George with anything but life.

This sketch has no pretense of being definitive or closely biographical. If it has the aura of impudence that's the way it was. George once remarked, after a Don Quixote tilt with a blond windmill in the form of a charming girl,

"She has a little love for everyone and not a great deal for anybody."

Whether true of the girl or not, I feel that George had unconsciously mirrored himself in these words. I can lay no claim to a special access to his feelings—we merely had a healthy, extrovertial intimacy, born, to coin a phrase, of mutual interests. Excluding the members of his family the only man who could possibly be said to have enjoyed such a special affection from George was the late Bill Daly (the conductor, William Merigan Daly). This, also, was an enthusiasm we shared.

If I should ever be empowered with high trust in the government—a career which I have not yet ruled out for myself—I should move at once to appoint Leonore Gershwin as Secretary of Private Relations for the Fine Arts—an American equivalent, if I misunderstand the term correctly, of the British Home Secretary.

Her management of a household that included two such persistently creative men as George and Ira—not to mention a dizzy panorama of strange faces, and other familiar ones similarly afflicted with talent—was a test of all those qualities of feminine tact, sensibility and patience which existed, so far as my experience is a criterion, only in her. I am reminded of how much she could bear by the memory of one of those long nights at the Gershwins which found me, at two-thirty in the morning, prompted to make some impossibly stupid and uncalled-for remark.

Leonore really became angry and said, "Get out of this house!"

"All right," I said petulantly, rising and preparing

to leave. In the midst of buttoning my jacket I stopped, sat down and said, "I'm not going."

"Why?" she queried.

"Because I have no place to go."

She laughed, and I stayed for another two years.

It is impossible to write of George without a word, even if an insufficient one, about Ira. Theirs were talents that suffused and penetrated each other, paralleled and completed each other remarkably. Prior to his professional association with Ira, Gershwin's songs were rarely supplied with more than run-of-the-mind texts. The exceptions would be in favor of those he wrote with Irving Caesar and Buddy de Silva. Ira's curious whimsicality and dryness, the brilliant finish and cohesion of his lyrics were a definite stimulus to George. One could not tire of the clean detail and effortless smoothness (in their final effect) of his texts.

Together they were interested, as a point of departure, in treating a thought, in evolving an idea. In their best work there is no compromise with traditional song-writing effects, no evidence of contentment either with echoing a manner devised by someone else or duplicating a coup they had evolved themselves. In consequence, the brightness of Ira's thought acted as a spur to George's musical resources and produced many songs that departed from the conventions they had found. They also strongly influenced others.

Rhythmically and formally the flow of Ira's verse frequently conditioned the turn of George's melodic and harmonic ideas. There was such an instance—to recall one of the last—in George's treatment of "Our Love Is Here to Stay" (actually his last completed song). This has a curiously continuous line, a rather complex pattern. After first hearing it I complained of its lack of breathing space in the second eight bars, its too-long contours, uttering some very cogent—so I thought—reasons for my opinion. George spent two days trying to rephrase the melody and simplify the line, eventually returning to the original form of it. Ira was quite annoyed with me, and rightly.

Together with his fondness for etymology and poker, Ira paralleled George's diversity of talents with his own skill in painting, his excellent tennis, though the tonality of these expressions was quite a different one. He tipped with his own brilliant brush strokes the work of everyone with whom he collaborated, stimulating Harold Arlen, Vernon Duke and Phil Charig to produce songs that were distinctly different from those they did with other lyricists. Though one would have to capture many silences and economic remarks in talking with him, Ira was capable of such effects in conversation as he once produced at my expense. Some wordy discussion had resulted in my statement that I would forgive him only if he kissed my cassock, saying that I felt in a monastic mood that evening.

Ira's rejoinder was:

> "*Oscar is a masochist*
> *'Cause he wants his cassock kissed.*"

One of his strongest emotions was his pride in George's talent. He saw the humor of George in some Debussy preludes which I played for him, quite without such an intention, shortly after George's death. The prelude called "Hommage à S. Pickwick, Esq." with its quotation of "God Save the King" (which, to Ira, was inevitably "My Country, 'Tis of Thee") suggested the "Wintergreen for President" music from *Of Thee I Sing*, and the music-hallish middle section of "Minstrels" also aroused an echo of George in his mind.

There is unquestionably such a thing as a "Gershwin" style, but it is also true that the adaptability of the brothers varied that style almost at will, superbly. At the time the vogue for operettas in the Viennese manner was flourishing in New York ten years or so ago—when *Blossom Time*, the *Desert Song* and *Rose Marie* were successively present—they might easily have produced a superior one of the species if their minds had been turned to it. George had a fine flair in this direction, as the examples of the waltz from *Pardon My English* (at the end of the first act), "I Was Above Love" (a fox trot in *Treasure Girl* which cleverly suggested a waltz feeling in its melody) and the neglected verse of "Delicious" clearly show. Then there is a charming Viennese strain at the opening of the second act of *Let 'Em Eat Cake*, for which Ira supplied the choice:

> *"Blue, blue, blue,*
> *Not purple or green or yellow*
> *Not brown the color of Othello*
> *But blue, blue, blue."*

Some of this writing was stimulated by George's visit to Vienna (during the European trip that produced "An American in Paris"), when he heard again Oskar Straus's *Chocolate Soldier*, a work for which he had a great fondness, along with several of Lehar's. I frequently amused him by referring to the solo of Bess, "I Love You, Porgy," as "Porgy in Vienna." Together with Ira, he could view this tendency humorously as he did in "I'm About to Be a Mother," sung by Mary in *Of Thee I Sing*, a lusty and infectious waltz with satiric undertones.

In another direction, Ira and George continued the evolution of the Gilbert and Sullivan tradition with their three political operettas, *Strike Up the Band*, *Of Thee I Sing* and *Let 'Em Eat Cake*. The verse for the title song in the first of these has a trenchant, unmistakably mordant emphasis which no previous composer of American operetta could have conceived, let alone dared to join with a presumably martial refrain. Even more striking in its originality is the "Wintergreen for President" chorus from *Of Thee I Sing*, in which there is actually a feeling of social comment, a remarkable accomplishment in light music. The "Union Square" episode in *Let 'Em Eat Cake* is of the same genre. All of these are the direct product of collaboration with Ira, effects that neither of them could have accomplished independently.

When they were confronted with a situation in the Astaire-Rogers *Damsel in Distress* that permitted it, they produced a work in the madrigal style—"The Jolly Tar and the Milkmaid"—so deceptively authentic that most of those who heard it accepted it as seventeenth-century English. In the same film, there is a big robust tune, "Sing of Spring," which has the circumstance if not the pomp of Elgar.

But I particularly like to recall those fugitive and sometimes barely noticed numbers in the various musical shows which burst on tired Broadway ears with a crackle and spurt of electric originality. There was the "You Don't Know the Half of It Dearie Blues," from *Lady Be Good*, with its very fresh treatment of the blues, its interjected fragments in double tempo, its satiric quotation of a fragment from the "Rhapsody"; "The Lorelei," from *Pardon My English*, which never became popular because its text was too purple for radio, with its fine old-fashioned jazz tune and its allusions à la rag to Silcher's *Lorelei*; the rowdy "Sam and Delilah," from *Girl Crazy*; the life and personality of the background music for the "Walking the Dog" sequence in *Shall We Dance*—which George deliberately, and with superb effect, scored for only eight instruments as a private commentary on the plushy, overstuffed scoring favored by most Hollywood orchestrators; the spirited one-steps, particularly the Kernesque strain which gave such a charming spice to "Oh! Kay"; practically all the verses of his songs, a field in which he functioned with especial magic; the openings and closings of the acts in *Lady Be Good*,

Girl Crazy and the three political operettas, in which George and Ira could let their fancies flow and flood without thought of tune dimensions or "hit" necessities. Much better known, but no less original, was the rhythmic vocal counterpoint for "Mine" in *Let 'Em Eat Cake*, a device recently admired as brilliant when it reappeared in the Tommy Dorsey swing version of Irving Berlin's "Marie." The resemblance was in the arrangement, not in the song, which Berlin wrote a few years before "Mine." Neither the list nor my memory of it is exhausted by these few citations.

How pervasive this rich inventiveness and forceful spirit was is reflected in its effect on so alien a musician as Schoenberg, who spoke these eloquent words at a memorial broadcast:

"George Gershwin was one of this rare kind of musicians to whom music is not a matter of more or less ability.

"Music to him was the air he breathed, the food which nourished him, the drink that refreshed him. Music was what made him feel, and music was the feeling he expressed.

"Directness of this kind is given only to great men, and there is no doubt that he was a great composer. What he achieved was not only to the benefit of a national American music but also a contribution to the music of the whole world."

No one could doubt from what I have said here and done publicly how much I am devoted to Gershwin's music, or how much it has meant to me. But I find pitifully small solace in the other cliché panegyrics whose one unison refrain was: "But his music lives on." I detest this self-derived omniscience—the survival of music is not determined by such tea-leaf fortunetelling. No quantity of music could compensate for the loss of his corporeal presence, the cessation of his creative being—especially when we could have had both.

The Boys Are Marching

The Boys Are Marching

AARON COPLAND HAS RECENTLY emerged as a figure of some significance in American music on the strength of his "The Second Hurricane," the score for the Ballet Caravan's *Billy the Kid*, the "Outdoor Overture" and various movie scores. But for dozens of American composers of my generation Copland has had a potent influence completely unknown to the public, in its sphere unmatched by that of any other native musician of the time.

This had nothing to do with the music he has written. It was an influence almost detached from the fact that he was a composer.

It is well to recall that in the early twenties, when modern music was attracting more attention in America than it ever did before, or has since, the public interest was wholly confined to European products —American music itself was in complete disrepute. It is questionable, indeed, if disrepute is the right word— there was no public awareness that such music existed.

From time to time and for purely chauvinistic reasons, some pseudo-American work might be produced for a Washington's Birthday or an Independence Day program, but it was, invariably, ideologically hyphenated: German-American, as in the case of Chadwick and Hadley, Scandinavian-American, as MacDowell's, French-American (Loeffler and Griffes), and even in the lighter species, Irish-German-American, as Victor Herbert's. There was nothing personalized in this art, little that was really professional and less that was American.

Like the best men in the American orchestras of the time, the finest teachers and the most celebrated performers on the concert stage, the influences to which these men reacted were imported. It is not possible to speak of an old school of American composition, a tradition or a background—there existed nothing that was genuine, not even the embryo of an authentic literature. It was comforting for such critics as Finck, Krehbiel and Aldrich to be able to include a chapter about "American Composition" in their occasional books and point to these men, but they might as well have cited Reger, Elgar and Taneieff for all the relationship they had, actually, to the American scene.

Along with other young men of his time—Roy Harris, Robert Russell Bennett, Walter Piston, Quincy Porter and even George Antheil—Copland himself grew up under this European tradition. An American teacher sufficed for his early training, but he felt obliged to go abroad for his important influences. When he returned he was adept at his craft, eager for accomplishment, enthusiastic—and completely dislocated.

As a rallying point there was such a group as the League of Composers, founded in 1923, which sought to establish in the East Sixties an equivalent of the Parisian salons. It engaged in the wholesale production of new music and performed a valid and highly important service in introducing such works as Stravinsky's "Renard" and "Histoire du Soldat," Schoenberg's "Pierrot Lunaire," Hindemith's "Kammermusik"—and how much "Kammermusik!"—which were outside the scope of the average symphony and thus could not be heard elsewhere.

Since there was this enthusiasm, and a period of being influenced by these things, most of the native music produced by the league could be described as an echo of the louder, better-known pieces by Europeans. The American composers of the late twenties could almost be grouped into Stravinsky boys, Schoenberg boys, Hindemith boys—and, a little later, League-of-Composers or New-School-for-Social-Research boys, according to where the infrequent performances of their works least infrequently took place.

The typical "modern" concert of that era had qualities that entitle it to preservation in print, for I doubt that a time will again come when music will be written and performed as it was in the mystified mid-twenties. There was almost certain to be some piece on the program by Carl Ruggles, who may be identified as a member of the New England, or dirt-farmer, school of composers. I have a particularly fond recollection of his piece called "Angels," scored for six trumpets and played by a half-dozen bald Italians of indeterminate poundage from the Metropolitan Opera House orchestra. Indifferent to the surroundings and almost visibly contemptuous of the music they were present to perform, they went about their duties in a patronizing manner that portrayed more vividly than words how much they rather would be playing the "Triumphal March" from *Aïda*.

Ruggles was a composer who worked in the serial, or Rover Boys tradition, for in addition to "Men and Angels" (from which this was an excerpt), his output included an orchestral work entitled "Men and Mountains." I fully expected that the next concert would bring forth a work entitled "Men and Mice," but I never went back to find out.

Another regular at these festivities was Edgar Varese, a composer who I always suspected was subsidized by the Sargent Hardware Company. He scorned the use of traditional instruments and accepted combinations, preferring to write for eight wood blocks, gong and tam-tam; or trombone, bass drum, crash cymbal and theremin. A mathematician by training, Varese's music carried logic to a point of frenzy, with meticulously subdivided beats and rhythms for which the proper instrument of reference was not a metronome but an adding machine.

It was always a source of perplexity to me that his insistent propaganda to be considered an American composer (Varese did not come to this country until 1919, when he was thirty-four years old) did not include the use of English words in his titles. He preferred the fancy sound of "Amériques," "Espace," "Intégrales" and "Arcana." I believe his hour of greatest triumph came four or five years ago when he conducted his "Ionization"—scored for thirteen percussion players—in tiny Carnegie Chamber Hall, where even a pin dropping causes a clatter.

Other constituents of such a concert were the usual League-of-Composers piano sonata, in which the three middle octaves of the instrument were rigorously avoided, while the composer (who generally played the work himself, possibly because nobody else could) worked diligently at the extreme bass and treble. If the sonata was absent, its place was apt to be taken by something percussive by Henry Cowell. In this the keys of the piano were completely ignored while the composer inserted his head into the piano's innards and plucked masterfully at the strings, against an accompaniment on Indian thundersticks avidly operated by a disciple.

The accepted chamber music of these concerts was no less individual, for it ranged from canons for a quartet of bassoons to something light and gay for viola, harp, bass flute and contralto. The usual song was wordless, but if a text was used, it was something from the Chinese with a text translated either by Arthur Waley or Witter Bynner. Largely speaking, the greatest quantity of native music performed under these auspices was so lacking in individuality that I often wondered if the composer himself would recognize a piece as his own if he didn't know it was going to be played. The complete characterization of the average American "modern" work of that period was pronounced by an unregenerate listener who remarked, after hearing one, "It sounds like an accompaniment to something."

Together with the training he brought back from Paris, Copland returned with a vivid recollection of the manner in which the young French composers contrived to make themselves known—their allegiances and bickerings, their enthusiasms and disagreements. Money was still easy, and in an effort to attract a wider public than the League of Composers reached he promoted the support for a series of concerts at the Guild Theatre (the Copland-Sessions Concerts) in the boom year of 1928.

It was a trait of the music of this period that, along with the life of the times, it grew steadily more com-

plicated—rhythmically, harmonically, contrapuntally
—more difficult to perform and more difficult to ab-
sorb. Subconsciously, a composer had the feeling that
the more rehearsals a work required, the greater importance it assumed.

However, the economic developments after 1929
snuffed out much of this interest. The progress that
had been made toward insinuating new American
works into the programs of symphony orchestras was
arrested because the support of the orchestras was
dwindling, and the conductors did not wish to alienate
their audiences further by forcing difficult works on
them. Perhaps as a reflex of this there came a gradual
recession in the excesses of the music that was being
written, an attraction to simplicity, a reverence for
clarity as opposed to the former adoration of complexity. Not to be overlooked in this development was
a decrease in the patronage that had made the performance of involved scores possible, and which provided
the necessity for composers to revert to fundamentals
if they wanted their works to be played. The simple
life became an ideal in a composer's music as well as
in his personal habits.

Copland had attracted a good deal of attention in
esoteric circles during this decade, had a steady series

of performances of his works (the usual one, with each orchestra, of each work) and had eventually established a contact with Koussevitzky which virtually assured the production of his new scores as they were written. But, like the others of his generation, he found that a real contact with the public was beyond his reach, that American music was in an unbelievable condition of disrepute. The public was less than apathetic —it was, largely speaking, frankly hostile.

This attitude may to some extent have been a product of the music that was being written, but whatever its origin, it was certain to endure unless some means were taken to dissipate it. A new generation of composers was emerging which inevitably would be subjected to the same cycle of mild patronizing interest and essential indifference as that which preceded them.

Plainly the musical situation required the attention of some strong central figure who would put himself out to direct public attention to the talents of America's young composers, someone who would give them the encouragement of a friendly interest and, if possible, divert them from this cycle of exclusiveness which had been so mischievous an influence on the men of the preceding generation.

There was on the horizon no interested critic of sufficient influence to occupy the position of Edwin Evans, in England, Henry Prunières or Jean Cocteau in France, Guido Gatti in Italy or Stuckenschmidt, and Einstein in Germany—all of whom had a profound effect on the emerging new talents in their countries just before and after the war. The interested critics were not influential, and the influential critics were not interested. Lacking any other alternative, Copland projected himself into the situation, just to see what could be done about it.

It was about this time, early in 1932, that I first came into contact with him. The occasion was one of those miscellaneous evenings at the Gershwins'. Without benefit of training or pedagogy, I had begun to write a sonatina for piano. At George's suggestion, and with some slight coaxing, I played as much of it as I had written—the first movement. Copland listened and encouraged me to finish the work, saying that he would include it on the programs of the contemporary American music festival that he was organizing to take place in Yaddo, Saratoga Springs, that summer. With a definite objective thus provided, and stimulated by the interest of a composer of Copland's reputation, I enthusiastically resumed work on the piece.

Whether Copland had any genuine esteem for the

work or not, I could hardly say. I doubt very much if it could be called "his kind" of music. Certainly it wasn't learned, its foundation in jazz was an occupational rather than an intellectual trait, and it was devoid of profundity or significance. Nevertheless, there seemed to him a point in having the work completed, in projecting another musician even slightly along the road from tentative amateurism to professional status.

I must recount my impressions of that Yaddo interlude for several reasons. Added to my constitutional aversion to the country was the annoyance I had built up during the five-hour train trip, alone, from New York to Saratoga. I had no eye for the attractions of the mansion (which, I am informed, occupies handsome grounds adjoining the race track) and, indeed, the countryside was probably dark when I arrived. All that saved the situation, as far as I was concerned, was the presence of Russell Bennett, in a sense an interloper from Broadway as I was, but a musician of firm foundation and sound development, which I was not.

Before the concert we all sat down to dinner in an atmosphere whose preciosity exceeded anything in my experience. The air was full of jeer for everything and everyone outside the closed shop of those present. This startled me somewhat, and I was at a further disadvantage because I was the only one present who had not either studied in Paris with Boulanger or D'Indy or was not scheduled to leave for France as soon as the festival was over.

My work was to be given at the concert of that evening. Earlier in the day there had been a chamber-music program, in which (this being the flute period of American composition) George Laurent of the Boston Symphony played flute sonatas by Walter Piston and Henry Brant. Preceding my sonatina was a three-movement string quartet by Marc Blitzstein, which reflected one of the greatest presumptions toward an audience that I had ever encountered in any composer. Each of the movements was a largo, in which the contrasts were to be supplied by altered sonorities rather than a change in tempo. It was like a meal consisting entirely of stained glass, with different dressings.

Following this, my bright, entertaining, unweighty work (with its banal second movement) enjoyed a success particularly flattering because it was the first concert piece I had ever written. When it was over and I had retired to the off-stage room where the various composers were gathered, Blitzstein greeted me with the remark,

"Now try to write a little *music*."

I was delighted to discover that Copland was sufficiently human to put his own "Variations" last on this program, the only evening concert of the festival and consequently its most important. This was a departure from his usual self-effacement, and I mention it primarily for this reason. Further, it was a work already enshrined, as something of a legend, in the estimation of the devout—a legend with a halo. The reception of the score was so emphatic that it was repeated at the following morning's concert.

For that ceremony, however, I was not present. After the evening concert I went along to the home of a local music patron, where I heard the one work that impressed me during this whole visit. Ironically, it was nothing American, but a sonata by Alban Berg, played by Hortense Monath. It was more than a little bit romantic, and thus universally disliked by those present.

At this gathering were two remarkably unpleasant young men, truly possessed of a talent for inimicality —Jerome Moross and Bernard Herrmann. They were present to cast evil spells and mutter curses on everything that was heard at Yaddo, possibly because no works of theirs had been included. They were particularly contemptuous, in a frank and rather charming way, of me; as they interpreted the presence of my sonatina on the program as a cheap Copland trick to leaven the festival with "Broadway." The New England professors, Richard Donovan of Yale and Walter Piston of Harvard, who had much sounder critical background for a disparaging attitude, were altogether gentlemanly and pleasant.

The following morning stands out in my mind as one of the few times in my life I have gotten up at what, by conventional standards, is considered "early," to take the first train out of Saratoga before any more music was played. Under the spell of the surroundings, my subconscious impulse was to tell the cab driver: "To the next festival, please."

A week or so after my return I learned that my hasty exodus from Yaddo had deprived me of participating in perhaps the most important event of that whole festival, a conference of composers and visitors which took place after the Sunday concert. It was, according to the boys I spoke to afterward, the first public evidence of Copland's developing stature as a leader among the younger composers. He was present nominally as chairman of the meeting, but when it became apparent that the others in the group had merely jejune witticisms or spiteful personalities to articulate, he took charge of the discussion and really said some pertinent things.

By a helpful coincidence, the reporter of a local paper and also its music correspondent was present as observer for the Associated Press. He seized upon the most lurid remark in Copland's generally sensible discourse and put it on the wires for papers all over the country. In his reproduction, Copland was quoted as saying: "Frankly I consider newspaper criticism a menace. We would be better off without it."

Probably if Copland's strongly qualified statement had been reported accurately, it would have attracted no such attention as the garbled version did. It brought the festival attention in hundreds of newspapers which had ignored its musical significance entirely. Moreover, it permitted him a justifiable indignation for being misquoted and a legitimate demand for vindication. Thus he had his remarks widely reprinted verbatim, a right to which he would have had no claim otherwise.

I would like to reproduce some of the things he said, not only for their inherent truth, but also as an indication of how long these ideas have been in his mind. "Somehow," he said, "in America a composer is regarded as a menial, little place is reserved for him in the scheme of things. A composer friend of mine from abroad recently went with me to Carnegie Hall and as we walked through the corridor behind the boxes he said: 'I see pictures of Kreisler, McCormack and Paderewski, but why not Roger Sessions or Roy Harris?'

"Of course it's not merely a matter of having pictures in Carnegie Hall. But the attitude seems to be: 'He's there, so why worry about him?' That attitude is a result simply of the fact that for years American music was not very good and everybody knew it. But now the situation is different. Our composers have craftsmanship and the greater competence of their writing is a commonplace. Therefore, a new attitude toward it by the critics must be formed.

"A proof of this lack of interest among newspaper critics is their failure to attend this festival. They have no curiosity about new works that are being written. They feel, only, if a new work is written, all right, they'll go and hear it; if not, it satisfies them just as well. Such an attitude is annihilating; a composer can't write in a vacuum.

"But composers, in the face of these difficulties, must have assurance in their own value, must have the strength to fight the situation and change it. The feeling of being only tolerated must not weaken their courage; they must keep together in groups. Every group can function as it will, but our common purpose, common aspiration and common hope are only in a unity against the present bad situation."

As for the remark that precipitated the small flood of words in the press, it developed from a discussion of news values, and Copland's remark that a performance of *Andromache* in Württemberg had received more space in that day's New York papers than the domestic Yaddo festival. "Frankly," he said, "under such circumstances I consider daily newspaper criticism a menace, and we would be better off without it."

It is apparent from the sequence of these ideas that Copland's attitude was already formulated, seven years ago. Certainly much of his subsequent activity has been consistent with what he felt the need to be then as far as the American composer was concerned.

The principal outcome of this whole experience for me was that I began another piece. But, even more basically, I was affected by my contact with the slightly tarnished Ivory Tower attitude reflected by most of the composers I had met. To paraphrase Pirandello, they seemed a group of "Six Composers in Search of An Influence"—somewhat disturbed whether their next work should be in the line of Stravinsky's "Symphonie des Psaumes" (then much in the air) or along the lines of the Mexicans Revueltas and Chavez. There was precious little talk, or little precious talk, of "Gebrauschsmusik" (that is, "useful" or "functional" music) such as Hindemith and Weill were then producing in Germany.

There seemed to me a good possibility of another Yaddo festival in the next year, and an opportunity to have another piece played. After I had been working on it for some time, Copland came to my place one day, and I began to play it for him. He characterized it, after hearing a dozen bars of the first movement, as "A cross between Scriabin and Berg." When he left I tore it up. I liked it, though.

Ironically, I had started as an authentic American composer, writing out of my practical knowledge, and using jazz materials. It was no time at all, however, before I, too, was caught up in the "European tradition," producing derivative works with enthusiasm and labored facility.

One of them I wrote several years later, and it again resulted in a contact with Copland. It was the outcome of a little group of which I was a member, whose leitmotiv was bad manners. The other founding spirit

were the two bad boys of Yaddo, Moross and Herrmann. I was not writing many songs at this time (about
1934) but paid daily calls at Harms to sneer at everyone who had hits. I was then bitten by the virus that
nothing good could be successful, transmitted to me
from Herrmann, who also had contacts, but no business, at Harms.

Herrmann's ambition to become a conductor
gnawed at him so ferociously that he persuaded the
excellent orchestrator and composer Hans Spialek to
underwrite a series of concerts for him in Town Hall,
to be given by a chamber orchestra. Finding that my
"Broadway" tendencies did not preclude a sympathetic response to his brashness, Herrmann suggested
that I write a piece for these programs. I protested
that I had never written anything for orchestra, but
he summoned all of his peculiarly inarticulate per-
suasiveness to convince me that orchestration was a
push-over. He gave me daily pep talks, complete with
brief biographical sketches of composers who became
famous overnight on the strength of one piece. Then
he sent me a score, for study purposes, by one Max
Trapp (probably because it was the only one he had).
On my own, I purchased a small book on clefs. This
was my preparation for orchestrating.

When the orchestra was brought together and began to rehearse the sinfonietta I had written, I felt
much in the position of the character in Moss Hart and
George Kaufman's *Merrily We Roll Along*—a re-
creation of George Gershwin—who was given one of
Gershwin's most celebrated lines to speak:

"Sometimes what comes out of that piano frightens
me." In this case my emotions were provoked not by
inspiration but by incredulity.

Mine was the kind of a piece in which nobody knew
what was going on—including the composer, the conductor and the critics. Consequently I got pretty good
notices. The critics' attitude might in part have been a
reaction from the fact that Copland, part of whose
first symphony was included on the program, indignantly denounced the whole project during the intermission. Surrounded by an attentive group of disciples, he tiraded eloquently on the failings of the conductor, the meager talents of the orchestral players
and the presumption of both in playing difficult contemporary music. However, Herrmann has since justified his undertaking in many ways. Thus the other
composers on the program had the benefit of his pro-
tests when the critics came to write their reviews.

A year or two later I attended a meeting of composers at Town Hall, at which the speakers were Deems Taylor, Virgil Thomson and Copland. In a rather surprising and contradictory way the three men summed up the types of music being written in America at the time, and also the divergent attitudes of composers toward their craft.

Though I know little about Thomson's music—not being ascetic enough to appreciate choral music—I am a great admirer of his wit, his light touch as a writer and his thoroughly becoming artificiality. On this occasion he debunked the conscious "Americanism" of American music very effectively, mingling amusement with sharp good sense.

Whatever may be said of Thomson's quality as a composer, it will be recorded in the future that his *Four Saints in Three Acts* was an historic event in American music. It brought the American composer for the first time into the commercial theater; and, moreover, with a work of considerable commercial appeal. To be sure, he had the advantage of a collaborator named Gertrude Stein; but curiosity trade alone would not have sustained the work as long as it ran. Some part of that success was definitely the contribution of Thomson, in his creation of a truly delightful theatrical atmosphere, in the lilt and flow of the music, and, above all, with the demonstration once again of his superlative ability in the setting of English words.

From the success of *Four Saints* came the permanently organized Negro chorus which figured so importantly in *Porgy and Bess;* and likewise there came Alexander Smallens, who conducted both works. In sequence there came, too, the opportunities to work in the theater for many other American composers.

Taylor's contribution to the meeting was a vigorous, entertaining talk on the need for the composer to assert himself, to be self-reliant and independent. It was synonymous with his pragmatic approach to composition. Moreover, it was stimulating for the composers to be encouraged by a man of Taylor's numerous contacts.

The realistic, practical side of the matter was presented by Copland, who was a little bitter, in words as stark and unadorned as his own orchestration. He talked emphatically about the need for organization, especially to impose a system of fees for performance rights on orchestras, choral organizations and even recitalists using American material. It seemed to me that the position of the American composer was decidedly a paradoxical one—to be demanding performance fees when conductors were reluctant to play their works at all. But Copland insisted on the need for establishing a precedent, even at the risk of losing performances.

The same meeting was repeated later in California, but recast, with Hollywood composers. Copland again had the leading role, supported by Louis Gruenberg and Joseph Achron. Present also at this meeting was Arnold Schoenberg, whom I chauffeured around from place to place. Often on these trips I would exchange his ideas with him.

Properly to define the atmosphere of this occasion, I must add that I had begun to work seriously at composition during the four or five elapsed years since Yaddo. When Copland reached California, I asked him to look at some of my things. Beguiled by my small promises of jobs (eventually unfulfilled), four studio musicians had consented to learn my quartet. When they played it for Copland, he expressed his pleasure with the progress I had made in the formal aspects of composition, his approval of the seriousness in the work, the good contrapuntal structure and solidity of the writing. After that he got critical—a formal word for captious and piddling—particularly about the harmonic style, which he termed excessively chromatic.

Since I had no capacity for anything but fulsome admiration, I felt that his remarks should be disqualified as intellectual hitting below the belt. My first instinct was to respond that his "Variations" were completely lacking in harmonic style, and full of dissonant clichés (especially those empty diminished ninths). In a further juvenile annoyance, I ran off to Schoenberg, building, as I went, a complete case *contra Copland*. With elaborate embroideries I outlined a Copland who had practically demolished Schoenberg, with my work as a mere pretext.

Schoenberg, it is well to know, is quick to defend himself even when he is not attacked. His appearance at the meeting therefore could hardly be described as a new high in amiability. Since I had also imposed my flair for the quarrelsome on Louis Gruenberg—who, as it chanced, was the host for the occasion—the air was quivering with temperamental electricity. Copland could not understand the reason for Schoenberg's formal but distant manner, not knowing of course that I had "run to teacher" with my tattle-taling.

After the meeting dispersed, I contritely took Copland to the most expensive restaurant in Hollywood, where I illuminated him on the cause for Schoenberg's coldness. He was justifiably furious with me. Nevertheless, when this same quartet was performed on a League of Composers broadcast last year it was wholly because of Copland's recommendation.

I saw a good deal of Copland in Hollywood at that time, while he was working on his "Music for Radio," for the Columbia Broadcasting System's Composers' Commissions. Whether he had any direct responsibility in the establishment of these yearly commissions—which have been of great service to some of our most talented men—I can't say, but I am sure that his agitation for American music, his constant propagandizing was a motivating factor. Also he was largely responsible for directing one of these commissions last year to Jerome Moross with the considerable assistance of Bernard Herrmann.

Moross was also in Hollywood at the time, and together with me presented an informal evening of Copland's music at the Antheils'. (Sunset Boulevard was practically the Boul' Mich of American music at that time.) On the program was a four-hand version of Copland's "El Salón Mexico," which he played with Moross, and Aaron's—or to borrow Antheil's pronunciation, Ay-ron's—early piano concerto, in which I took part. I enjoyed this evening enormously, even if

the jazz figurations of the concerto (which was written in 1926) now sound dated and corny.

One of my most pleasant recollections of the occasion was the zealous and undeviating loyalty of Moross
to Copland. This was emphasized by his unfailing
habit of remarking, with a wide and pleased grin, about
any new work that was played: "That's a baad piece."
This applied to anything from Debussy to Schoenberg, always, of course, excluding Copland. I recall
one instance when a composer—a superficial Paul
Whiteman composer (Chaminade with brass) of the
"Got Them There Blues Again" school—played a
new conceit for us. Moross seemed surprised when he
rendered his inevitable judgment—"That's a baad
piece"—that the composer didn't agree with him.

I only mention this because Moross is a lad of genuine talent whose career, from public and high school
in Brooklyn, through the Juilliard and out (in brief
time) is an example of the difficulty that confronts a
youngster in this country who wants to be a composer.
His family could see no business future in serious composing, and insisted that he spend his time practising
the piano. Naturally he rebelled against this as soon as
he was able to care for himself. However, his lack of
commercial adaptability made his life difficult. Proba-

bly, too, the combination of these factors was responsible for some of that malevolence and captiousness which I have noted. I have faith in his talent, however, and believe that it will eventually orientate itself.

While they were in Hollywood, Copland and Moross had the usual lunch with Boris Morros of Paramount, who thereafter released the usual stories to the press, about the movies encouraging serious composers, American as well as foreign. However, as he had in those other instances, he forgot to offer Copland and Moross jobs.

When I had *my* lunch with Boris Morros, he mentioned with casual impressiveness that he had had breakfast with Sibelius, a lunch with Ravel and dined with Prokofieff.

When I responded: "It sounds like an ad for Imperial Airways—breakfast in Finland, lunch in Paris and dinner in Leningrad"—my future with Paramount was sealed, and how tightly.

Considering that I am a person who lacks no possible human failing, I have been constantly amazed by Copland's generosity. Encountering a particular example of it one day, I said to him in wonder and curiosity,

"Weren't you ever jealous of anyone?"

His reply was, "When I first went to Paris I was jealous of Antheil's piano playing—it was so brilliant; he could demonstrate so well what he wanted to do."

Since Copland went to Paris first in 1921, it is apparent how far back he had to look for a jealousy.

I did not see Copland again after that for some time, until possibly two years ago, when the same Composers' Meeting took place in New York once more, at the Professional Musicians' Club, which had clubrooms on the roof of the Ziegfeld Theatre. Since I had been at the meeting twice before, I missed it this time, arriving after the discussion for the particular purpose of seeing Copland. Here I met all the young men of the newest group of American composers, those who had been spared the difficulties of the dark ages B.C.—Before Copland.

One of them particularly impressed me with his rather engaging toughness—the red-headed forthright young David Diamond. When I asked Copland what kind of music he wrote, he replied enthusiastically,

"Streamlined!"

This was rather baffling to me, but I discovered Diamond to be a youngster of exceeding practicality. For a composer now only twenty-four, he had written an astounding quantity of music, including a sinfonietta and a symphony, a violin concerto, a harpsichord concerto, a cello sonata, a chamber symphony, a trio, a quartet, a ballet and so on. Among his teachers had been Bernard Rogers, Sessions, Boepple and Boulanger. Nevertheless, just before he received a Guggenheim Fellowship in composition this year he was working as a soda jerker.

From the things Copland talked about that he was busy with at the time I could not fail to be impressed with how much the situation had altered since that first summer at Yaddo. His score for the radio had just been performed, and he was even then in the midst of a competition designed to produce a new title for the work. Appeals had been made for listeners to submit a suggestive name to replace the formal "Music for Radio." To Copland's surprise, the piece had distinctly Western overtones for a good many of his listeners, the winning title, eventually, being "Saga of the Prairee."

This adaptation of a commercial device (almost suggesting that Copland was affiliating himself with "Lucky Strike" or "Old Gold") was evidence of a digression toward practicality that had begun to assert itself in American music generally at this time. In Copland's output it was further exemplified by his *The*

Second Hurricane, a dramatic and musical work for high-school children that was first given at the Neighborhood Playhouse on Grand Street, in New York, in 1937. No doubt this undertaking was founded on Copland's realization that music instruction in the high schools of the country had expanded enormously in the last generation, and that an excellent market existed for choral and orchestral music that could be performed by youngsters. Certainly he could anticipate for this score a wider circulation than for anything he had previously written.

As well as being a shrewd summation of a need, it provided Copland with an impetus that produced music of fine directness and clarity, possessed of a humor and good nature that had never been considered traits of his style. It was what might be called a "happy" work, written to be performed, and thus conceived in a different spirit than something which the composer fears may remain unheard for a dozen years, or forever.

Subsequently, as I noted before, Copland wrote another bright and spirited piece also for high-school performance—his "Outdoor Overture," whose première occurred only last winter. Among his other recent works have been a rhythmic and highly individualized score for *Billy the Kid* and his movie music for the World's Fair film, *The City*. Indeed, as far as I know he has not recently written anything other than commissioned works. This suggests that Copland was determined to make his talent work for him; and perhaps even to his own surprise discovered that there was both a market and an audience for his products. It is a significant thing, too, that the quality of all this music has been very clean and high.

Among those others who were present at Yaddo when Copland delivered his protest against composing in a "vacuum" it is pertinent to observe that Marc Blitzstein in particular has found a valid use for his talent. Not, to be sure, in writing largos for string quartet, but in writing both the text and the music of that astounding success *The Cradle Will Rock*. It was not only widely admired and a fine source of income both for Blitzstein and the Mercury Theatre which took it over when the WPA begged to be excused; it was also an event of salutary importance in Blitzstein's life. For the first time, probably, he realized that he had the capacity to be successful, which gave him virtually a fresh grasp on his career. This work and its companion opera for radio *I've Got the Tune*, certainly brought him a wider prominence and a deeper personal satisfaction than all the concert music he had written in the previous fifteen years.

As a reflection of Blitzstein's literary talent, I found the libretto of "The Cradle Will Rock" surprisingly unsubtle and heavyhanded, since his writings in *Modern Music* and other publications had impressed me as the work of a literate, perspicacious and lacerating critic of music. In the text there was an old-fashioned 1902 Bowery toughness—the streetwalker leaning against the prop lamp saying huskily: "Got a match, buddy?"—that reminded me of a Paul Armstrong play. Its pseudo-virility I felt to be forced and artificial.

On the other hand, I found the musical settings highly ingenious and persuasively rhythmic, with some bright flashes of amusing comment in the piano accompaniment. As for Blitzstein's own performance at the piano, his skill in delivering the verbal commentary that kept the show going, it was an executive tour de force which contributed much to the quality of the evening, and really vitalized its appeal as a theatrical production.

The considerable réclame the work enjoyed, the wide and controversial comment that it stimulated was a provocative influence on Blitzstein's contemporaries. It opened a vista of new opportunities for them, suggesting uses for their talents that had not previously occurred to them. This view was substantiated by Blitzstein himself when I met him, flushed by the kudos of a Broadway success in the Stork Club. Between rhumbas he told me,

"There's no future for the American composer in writing music for Carnegie Hall. His hope lies in writing music that is intimate, entertaining, accessible —that reaches an audience directly, like a ballet or a theatrical score."

This pronouncement hardly pleased me, since I had just begun to write a cantata on *Rasselas* by Dr Samuel Johnson (as a preparatory exercise for setting Carlyle's *The History of the French Revolution*) scored for a large chorus, an orchestra of one hundred fifty and military band.

However, the sound sense of Blitzstein's contention cannot be denied. Virtually all the activity in American music recently has been in places other than the concert hall. Our composers are beginning to realize that, just as the Parisian composers of the last generation—from Stravinsky and Prokofieff down through Ravel, Milhaud, Poulenc, Honegger, Auric and the others—first came to prominence through the ballet, so the theater (in which may also be included the ballet and films) offers them a rich opportunity to earn a living, perfect their craft and acquire a following.

In addition to Copland, Robert McBride, Elliott Carter, Jr and Virgil Thomson have recently written scores for the Ballet Caravan; Paul Bowles has done scores for the Federal Theatre (*Horse Eats Hat*) and the Group Theatre (*My Heart's in the Highlands*); Lehmann Engel wrote the admired music for last season's *American Landscape*; Paul Nordoff has filled a number of commissions for Katharine Cornell; and to revert to Copland again, his theater assignments have included scores for *The Five Kings* and *Quiet City*. For my own part, I have had employment both in writing music and conducting for *The Fabulous Invalid* and *The American Way*, and similar duties with the puppet short film for the Petroleum Industry's exhibit at the World's Fair. The latter has also provided a fine stimulation to the talent of Russell Bennett, who wrote the excellent scores for its fountain exhibits, and for William Grant Still, who wrote a score, on commission, for the Democracity.

On other fronts, too, there have been equal portents of an expanding independence for the American composer. The bewildered Henry Brant has emerged from his flute period of Yaddo and made use of his musical skill to make a fine arrangement for Benny Goodman of Alec Templeton's "Bach Goes to Town." Even Roy Harris has descended from his medieval stronghold to write a symphony for the swing band of the amiable Tommy Dorsey, who thereafter retired to his spacious estate in New Jersey for two weeks to contemplate the vagaries of life.

After serving an apprenticeship in insolence, Bernard Herrmann has steadily increased his skill as a conductor to the point where he is a valued member of the staff at WABC (of the Columbia Broadcasting System), incidentally finding time to write a cantata on Melville's *Moby Dick* which the Philharmonic has scheduled for this season.

One of the most important factors in this regeneration, if one of the most obscure, has been the Federal Music Project of the WPA with its Composers' Forum Laboratory, as well as its formal concerts. Not only in New York but in many other cities through the country it has provided an agency for that most important of all services to the composer—an opportunity to hear how his music sounds. Regardless of how large or how small the audiences have been, it has fulfilled an essential function for the composer, and, in a number of instances, reminded some of them that they are composers.

One of the most stimulating experiences I have ever had in a concert hall was the recent evening in New York, jointly sponsored by the Guggenheim Foundation and the WPA, devoted to music by composers who have held Guggenheim Fellowships. Regardless of one's reaction to the individual merits of the works by William Schuman, Copland, Piston, Harris and Nordoff, one could not be indifferent to the skill and professionalism of virtually everything that was heard, or immune to the repeated expressions of enthusiasm from the audience.

It was my feeling that this survey should conclude, as a movie producer instructed the writers who were preparing a screen version of Dostoievsky's *Crime and Punishment*, on "a note of hope." But it does not need to be artificially created. It is implicit in the renewed energy with which American composers have set about their work, on the basis of even the slight encouragement I have outlined; in the firmer tone and more positive spirit of the scores they are creating; in the evidence, in some directions at least, that they are no longer unwanted.

The road ahead is still a rough one; but the boys are marching.

con sordine

con sordine

THERE'S A GREAT STORY IN ME IS ALWAYS
a conviction of amateur writers (like myself) who
recognize their disqualifications for the status of
author but nevertheless have been cajoled into writing
books. There's never been a great story in me. As you
have no doubt discovered by now, my adventures
have been wholly undramatic, strictly of the *Kaffee-
klatsch* type. Therefore when I was approached by a
publisher to write a book I replied hastily, and with
one of the few rare flashes of absolute clarity I have
ever experienced, that my opinion on all subjects was

equally unimportant. The publisher's agent (I dislike "my" publishers as an impertinence) said,

"Would you write a book about Victor Herbert?"

"Write one?" I exclaimed in reply. "I wouldn't even read one."

This implies no disrespect for Victor Herbert's music but merely reflects my conviction that he is not a composer to write about or read about. (I trust that Deems Taylor, who has written a fine tribute to Victor Herbert in *The Music Lovers' Encyclopaedia*, a book published by "my" publishers, will not regard this personally.)

The irony of the offer was that even before I had written a line I was in the position of rejecting a publisher. It occurred to me that there must be dozens of men who had written out of conviction and an inner struggle books that were not being published. I felt it almost as an insult that I, whose experience in writing had been limited to a career as a dilatory correspondent, should be asked to write a book in preference to one of these.

The truth then seeped out. Due to an accidental circumstance* by which my impertinence had become

---

*It was in the summer, and nobody was in town when Dan Golenpaul, producer of "Information Please," needing a fourth for his tournament of occasional information, approached me.

a salable product, coupled with a widespread misconception that I was infallible in musical knowledge,
an undercover demand had arisen for a volume with
my name on it. That misconception, I might add,
flourished exclusively among people largely ignorant
of music. Most persons professionally engaged in
music, who had been reared in a musical atmosphere,
would qualify as well to answer the average questions
that are asked. The questions, generally speaking, are
taxing only to a layman's knowledge of music, not a
musician's.

However, a legend—so easily started—induces its
own complications. I was enjoying a quiet lunch at a
hotel with Fritz Reiner recently when he suddenly
directed my attention to music from the loud-speaker
in the dining room, and said,

"You're supposed to know everything. What's
that?"

This suggestion that I was incapable of error was
only slightly more nettling than my realization that
the music of the moment was hardly more than unfamiliar. At length it aroused some echo, and I said,
"Smetana." Then as an obvious corollary (since it is
practically the only work of his that is ever played)
I said, "From the *Bartered Bride*."

Reiner, who knows the whole score from memory, had to start with the overture and review the work scene by scene until he reached the third act and corroborated me by saying,

"You're right. It's the 'Dance of the Comedians.'"

After the initial exchange of opinions with the publisher there ensued an interlude in the negotiations, during which the liaison man continued his coquetry, calling me after each broadcast and praising me without stint. Then he would add suggestions how I could utilize in a book this or that morsel of information which had been elucidated on the night before's program. Not to be subtle about it, his praise made me ecstatic. Within a few weeks he had collected a volumeful of suggestions.

These suggestions had the force of creating a concise nebula, replacing what had hitherto been a dispersed confusion. The chaos was resolved when he appeared flourishing a paper that contained the solution to my dilemma—a check for advance royalties. I said, "What's that?"—grasping at it with a clutch that indicated a complete lack of uncertainty in my mind.

I realized that I had maneuvered myself inadvertently into a better bargain than I could have driven intentionally. It recalled to me the experience of Max

Gordon and Noel Coward when that producer was negotiating for the right to *Design for Living*. Coward exacted such terms from Gordon that someone commented:

"Only an artist could drive such a bargain.
A businessman wouldn't have the nerve."

It should also be understood that this check opened up a new vista to me. No contemporary composer—with the exception perhaps of Richard Strauss or Maurice Revel—has made a living out of his music. Schoenberg has written a famous treatise on composition and teaches. Stravinsky learned to play the piano and conduct, after making a reputation as a composer, in order to increase his income by personal appearances. Prokofieff tours as a pianist and also conducts. Rachmaninoff, of course, is even more celebrated as a virtuoso than he is as a composer. Hindemith has played in a quartet and makes appearances as a solo violist. Sibelius lived for years—before his music was played as generally as it is now—on the government subsidy which is still a comfort to him today.

Among American composers, Aaron Copland writes books, lectures and talks on the radio. Roy Harris and Roger Sessions teach, as do Walter Piston, Robert McBride, Douglas Moore, William Schuman and

Bernard Wagenaar, to mention at random a few names that come to my mind. In England, Constant Lambert does a great deal of conducting and has written an excellent book entitled *Music Ho!* Eugene Goossens, whom the English consider one of their representative composers, is permanent conductor of the Cincinnati Orchestra.

I don't mean to identify myself with such men, but if the problem is acute for them, how much more so was it going to be for me? Even patrons and patronesses are not much help, for the cultivation of them is an occupation even more exacting than trying to earn a living. Also, their interest is much overrated. Most of them prefer horses.

Perhaps the only *bona fide* offer of patronage I ever had came some years ago in Pittsburgh when a local enthusiast suggested that I should go abroad to Paris, offering to finance a year's stay with Prokofieff. I replied that I would be glad to go abroad and spend a year with Prokofieff, if, at the end of the year, Prokofieff would come back and spend a year with me in Pittsburgh.

I didn't actually meet Prokofieff until a year or so ago when he came into the office of Chappell's (the publishers) one day to get a score of Gershwin's

Porgy and Bess to take back with him to Soviet Russia. With a memory still strong of his muscular playing (especially of the third piano concerto) I pleaded with Prokofieff to play the theme of the second movement for me. When he finally sat down at the piano he confessed that he didn't remember it clearly, and I helped him pick out the notes as he stumbled through it rather awkwardly.

It was thus as a way to make composing possible that the writing of this book appealed to me. I have observed among some of the men who have sought to develop profitable avocations that an element of pride makes its appearance sooner or later. Desiring to execute the work of their choice the best way possible, they discover that the pursuit of excellence eventually takes up more time than composing.

However, it is not likely to be so with my writing. I discovered, soon after concluding the necessary negotiations with the publishers, that one of the concomitants of the association was a flow of excellent books that they published. Whether this graciousness was purely altruistic or whether it was designed to stimulate me by calling to my attention subtlely the quality of the books on their list, I still have not discovered. I do know, however, that the first of

[257]

them—Edna Ferber's *A Peculiar Treasure*—reached me just after I had started work on my first chapter. Her absorbing material and smooth manipulation of it engrossed me for two weeks, effectively distracting me from any further concentration on my task.

When I returned to writing again I consoled myself with the feeling that my enterprise would go better after I had gotten into it more. This process was proceeding apace when the publication date for Vincent Sheean's *Not Peace But a Sword* rolled around, and the volume duly appeared in my mail. I can heartily recommend this as a brilliant examination of recent events in Europe, as a magnificent piece of journalism, especially the moving chapter devoted to James Lardner. But, as a diversion, as home reading for an amateur engaged in writing his first book, it is definitely to be shunned.

This mood endured for a while, until it occurred to me that Sheean's material was the outgrowth of a personal contact with important, world-shaking happenings abroad, that it was in no way an analogue with my undertaking. Cheered, I returned to work again. Hardly had I done so when the considerable bulk of Somerset Maugham's *Teller of Tales* was deposited on my doorstep. The grace and vividness of Maugham's own twenty-six page preface was but an initial disturbance. There were still the hundred-odd stories in the volume to consider, which I did at length, though at hardly a rate of more than one a day.

Fortunately, my contract had been executed in the late spring, and when these books had been released there ensued a respite from important publications during the remainder of the summer. Had the negotiations begun in the fall, with a whole winter's supply of books coming to me free, it is doubtful indeed if this volume would ever have been concluded.

However, as my own total of words and lines began to mount I became aware, more and more, of my identity with Tommy Dorsey's attitude toward a radio program on which we both played some years ago. This was an hour which used an orchestra conducted by the late Bill Daly. Among the members of the orchestra were Benny Baker, who is now first trumpet of the NBC orchestra under Toscanini, and Benny Goodman, who is now Benny Goodman. The tenor that Daly used married a Madame Butterfly in a touring opera company who was really a Japanese. Everything happened on this program.

Despite the presence of Goodman and Dorsey the orchestra played no real jazz and little popular music of any kind, unless you consider the "Kashmiri Love Song" or "In a Persian Garden" popular music. We also played the standard overtures, Liszt's "Hungarian Rhapsodies" and operatic excerpts.

It chanced that on the first program that Dorsey played, Daly had a baritone soloist (a young singer named Nelson Eddy) who wanted to sing Iago's "Credo" from *Otello*. As those who have heard the opera know, the entrance of the singer is preceded, and his discourse is several times punctuated, by impressive chords from the trombones, with one solo instrument particularly prominent. To Dorsey, because of his reputation in the profession, fell the honor of filling the first chair and playing the exposed passages. Anxious to do the job up brown, he rose from his chair and began to play the music with a broad, mellifluous tone, meanwhile fluttering his right hand rapidly on the slide to give each note the maximum of throbbing, vibrating "schmaltz."

"No, no," cried Daly in horror. "Not that way."

"Sorry," said Dorsey phlegmatically, "that's the way we do it at Roseland."

So, in a sense, this book is written "the way we do it at Roseland." There is no literary parallel for the difference that is implied in the mention of the Roseland Ballroom against the Metropolitan Opera House, but if there were one it would suit my purpose precisely.

My first impulse was to fill up as many pages as possible and get the thing over, like a bad dream. Then when the editor suggested that this or that episode was not so good my only impulse was to protest indignantly,

"But it fills up two more pages!"

I also developed a fondness for conversational writing, after I discovered that if you wrote—My answer to her query was "No"— it did not take up nearly as much space as writing:

"What is your answer?" she asked.

"My answer," I replied, "is no."

These purely mechanical problems soon adjusted themselves. However, the problem of writing about music has been complicated recently by the outpouring of books on the subject, especially those which profess to substitute the action of the eye for the function of the ear. These are the books of the genre known as "appreciation" and include such titles as "How to Listen to Music," "What to Listen for in Music," "What Not to Listen for in Music," "How to Understand Music," "What to Wear While Listening to Music," and so on. The thesis here is that every scrap of information bearing upon a symphony, a tone poem, an overture or a concerto, when added together, will total a sum of knowledge equal to the one thing that the reader lacks: a liking for music.

The attitude expressed in these books reminds me of the rather naïve query of a musically well-versed person who once said in great mystification to Toscanini,

"Tell me, maestro, how do you learn all those scores from memory?"

Toscanini looked at him gruffly and answered, "I learn them."

I have often wondered what happens to a listener so schooled when he hears a work about which nobody knows whether the composer took a long walk in the garden between the first and the second movements, about which Ernest Schelling has not exposed a series of lantern slides or Olga Samaroff-Stokowski delivered a long informative talk. He must certainly say to himself,

"The music sounds all right, but how about the lecture?"

I do not ignore the fact that during the last generation music has gone through a transition. From being hardly more than a subject for romantic novels—as far as the general public is concerned—it has progressed to the point where Iturbi makes jokes on the radio, and Leopold Stokowski's hands are almost as familiar to the movie public as Norma Shearer's. It has gotten so that a youngster proferring his talents to the Juilliard in exchange for a scholarship may anticipate being asked, after he had played Beethoven's "Hammerklavier" sonata,

"Very good. But how do you read lines?"

That is the case with pianists and violinists. With a singer (if of the female order) future success revolves not around her voice, style, musicianship or interpretative ability, but, rather, whether she is *photogénique*. As for the male, there is less concern with his potentialities as Wotan or Rhadames, Germont or Lohengrin, than there is with the question:

"Is he too short to play opposite Jeanette Mac-Donald, or too tall for Lily Pons?"

Moreover, when the summer bowls feel a deficit coming on they do not send out for a score of Mahler's "Resurrection" symphony, but, instead, make every effort to contact Lily Pons, Jascha Heifetz (star of *They Shall Have Music*) or Nelson Eddy. Any one

[263]

of them would sign away a week's receipts for the privilege of presenting Deanna Durbin.

All of this obviously has nothing to do with music *per se*. It has to do with an audience created by radio and pictures. The reactionary character of this audience may be demonstrated by the fact that the biggest song-hit writer of the year—with two tunes contesting for high position on the Hit Parade—was Peter Ilyitch Tschaikowsky ("Moon Love" and "Our Love"). In the instance of the first he was aided and abetted by André Kostelanetz. When Tschaikowsky's distinguished, but belated collaborator appeared at the Stadium this summer to lead the "Romeo and Juliet" overture there were more than a few of the assembled 22,000 (Lily Pons also sang) who regarded this as a particularly characteristic Kostelanetz arrangement of "Our Love." "Wait until next year," they said to each other, "when he does the 'Moon Love' symphony."

I do not think the future of music lies in this direction.

Neither do I think there is serious hope of creating a musical audience out of people who are enthusiastic about Gilbert and Sullivan. I am aware that this is generally spoken of as "a great tradition," but it is largely so among unmusical people. I have never encountered anyone who derived genuine pleasure from Mozart's *Marriage of Figaro* who actually became ecstatic about *The Pirates of Penzance*, or an enthusiast for Smetana's *Bartered Bride* who would accept *The Mikado* as a substitute if he were presented with a choice between one or the other.

As for the unlimited thousands who bruised each other for the privilege of hearing Pons sing at the Stadium last summer, I doubt if there are 22,000 people in the whole country who are familiar with the name, merely, of a person infinitely more important to music in this country than Pons and Kostelanetz taken together. I am thinking of one of the greatest (because discriminating) patronesses of all time—Mrs Elizabeth S. Coolidge (no relation). The list of men she has commissioned to write chamber music is virtually a cross-section of the creative forces at work today—Stravinsky, Prokofieff, Schoenberg, Hindemith, Bartok, Piston, Pizzetti, Loeffler, Martinu are merely a few of the names. Moreover, she has introduced numerous fine European chamber-music ensembles to America—the Roths, the Pro Arte Quartet, the Busch Quartet, the Kolisches, among them—at her festivals in Pittsfield, paid for the playing of Beethoven quartet cycles (in

New York and California), donated an auditorium to the Library of Congress and otherwise spread her influence through the land.

It is true that the average concertgoer has no consciousness of her existence, but that is a matter of slight significance, I am sure, either to her or to those to whom her work is important—the composers. If this book had a little more dignity and substance I might be tempted to solve my dedication problem by inscribing it to Mrs Coolidge. However, this might be regarded as something of a sychophantic gesture, as if I were seeking the commission for a quartet in return. Frankly, as long as we're on the subject, I have no hesitation to say that I would have been more pleased to receive such a commission than to write this book. It would have been more in my line and would have involved nobody but myself, since few people would have heard it.

However, a good deal of what I know of music and also what I feel about it owes its origin to Sigismund Stojowski (please, *not* Stokowski) who is not only a brilliant pedagogue but a warmly sympathetic human being. The several years I spent studying piano in New York with him remain among the most profitable and worth remembering of my life. He provided the best summation of that period when he asked me what music I was going to play at a student recital for which he was preparing the program.

"I think I'll play Debussy's 'Reflets dans L'Eau' or 'Poissons d'Or,' " I answered.

He looked at me intently for a moment and then said,

"Your piano playing is not improving, but your French is."

Stojowski also unintentionally provided the best characterization of this volume when he said of Saint-Saens' G minor concerto,

"It begins with Bach and ends with Offenbach."

It is reported of Brahms that, on leaving a gathering one night where he had expressed his opinions with characteristic vigor and untrammeled candor, he turned and remarked, "If there is anybody here that I have forgotten to insult, I apologize."

Since I am not Brahms—and neither are you—I would like to apologize to all those I have not forgotten to insult.